Steady growth is expected despite headwinds

- Global economic growth was 3.2% in 2023, as economic activity showed resilience despite rising interest rates, and is projected to remain at this rate in 2024–2025. This is lower relative to historical performance as continued high borrowing costs, fiscal consolidation, muted productivity growth, lingering impacts of global shocks, and increasing constraints to trade and investment flows are all seen to limit expansion. Meanwhile, growth in developing Asia was 5.1% in 2023, driven by a resurgence in domestic demand. This is projected to be 5.0% in 2024 and 4.9% in 2025. Sustained expansion in South Asia and Southeast Asia, fueled by robust domestic demand and higher semiconductor and services exports, should offset moderating growth elsewhere in the region, including in the People's Republic of China (PRC).

- After expansion of 3.5% in 2023, the Pacific subregion is projected to grow by 3.3% in 2024 and 4.0% in 2025. Recovery of resource extraction in Papua New Guinea, stable visitor arrivals in most tourism-dependent economies, and stimulus from public infrastructure projects are seen to drive growth. However, this outlook has several downside risks, including labor shortages, reduced fiscal space, continued exposure to disaster risk, and volatility in global commodity prices and supply chains.

- The United States (US) economy grew by an annual rate of 1.3% in the first quarter (Q1) of 2024 compared to 3.4% in Q4 2023. The moderation reflected slower growth in consumer and state and local government spending and exports, as well as reduced federal government spending and increased imports. Growth is projected to be 2.0% in 2024 before slowing to 1.7% in 2025.

- In the PRC, gross domestic product (GDP) grew by 5.3% (year-on-year) in Q1 2024, slightly faster than the 5.2% growth realized in Q4 2023. Growth in high-tech manufacturing drove an expansion of 6.1% in industrial output. However, the continuing downturn in the real estate sector remains a challenge, with serious implications for consumer spending. The PRC economy is forecast to grow by 4.8% in 2024 and 4.5% in 2025.

- Japan's GDP declined by an annual rate of 1.8% in Q1 2024 after no growth in Q4 2023. Private consumption fell for the fourth straight quarter by 0.7%, as rising costs dampened demand. Private investments and net exports were also subdued, but government consumption and public investments increased. The Japanese economy is seen to grow by 0.6% in 2024, rising to 1.0% in 2025.

- The Australian economy remained flat in Q1 2024, recording annualized growth of 0.1% after 0.3% in the previous quarter. Household consumption increased during the period, as did government expenditure driven by increased spending on social assistance, energy bill relief payments, and national defense. Accumulation of inventories likewise contributed to growth. Offsetting these developments were declines in total investment, reflecting the winding down of recent mining and government projects, subdued property market activity, and increased merchandise imports. Growth is projected to be 1.4% in 2024, picking up to 2.3% in 2025.

Gross Domestic Product Growth (%, annual)

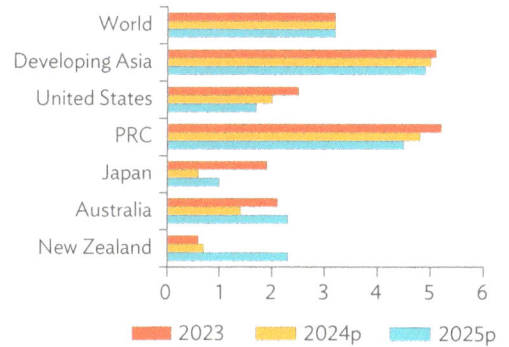

2023   2024p   2025p

p = projection, PRC = People's Republic of China.

Notes: As defined by ADB, developing Asia comprises the 46 of the bank's members in Asia and the Pacific. Figures are based on ADB estimates except for world GDP growth (IMF), and Australia and New Zealand (Consensus Economics).

Sources: *Asian Development Outlook* database (accessed 17 July 2024); Consensus Economics. 2024. *Asia Pacific Consensus Forecasts May 2024*; and International Monetary Fund. 2024. *World Economic Outlook: Steady but Slow: Resilience Amid Divergence* (April).

Gross Domestic Product Growth in Developing Asia (%, annual)

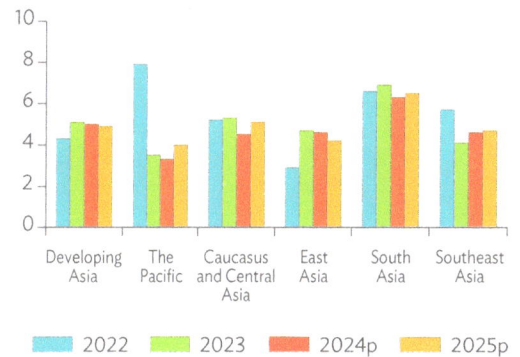

2022   2023   2024p   2025p

p = projection.

Note: As defined by ADB, developing Asia comprises the 46 of the bank's members in Asia and the Pacific.

Source: *Asian Development Outlook* database (accessed 17 July 2024).

Food Prices
(January 2022 = 100)

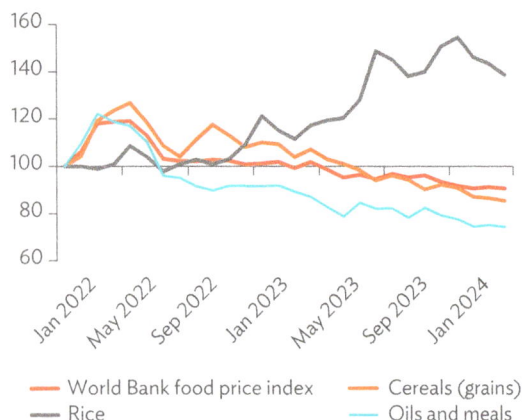

Source: ADB calculations using data from the World Bank. 2024. *World Bank Commodity Price Data* (Pink Sheet) (accessed 14 May 2024).

Prices of Selected Resource Export Commodities
(January 2022 = 100)

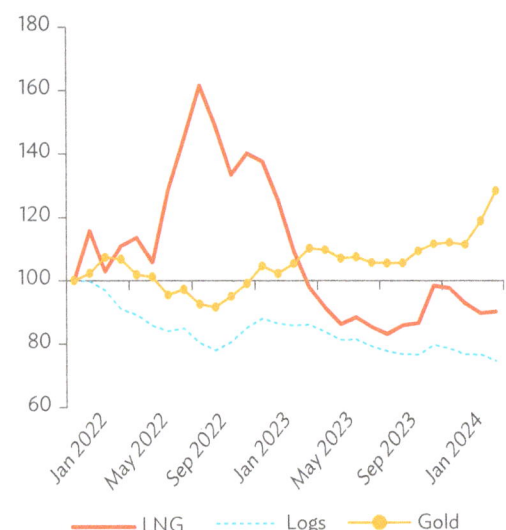

LNG = liquefied natural gas.
Source: ADB calculations using data from the World Bank. 2024. *World Bank Commodity Price Data* (Pink Sheet) (accessed 14 May 2024).

- New Zealand recorded a slight annualized growth of 0.2% in Q1 2024 compared with a 0.1% contraction in Q4 2023. Expansion in rental, hiring, and real estate services, as well as electricity, gas, water, and waste services, offset declines in construction, manufacturing, professional services, and public administration. On the expenditure side, private consumption rose by 0.8% as spending on services and non-durable goods increased, offsetting a 6.1% increase in imports—mainly of intermediate goods and goods for consumption—and a 1.3% decline in gross capital formation. The New Zealand economy is seen to grow by 0.7% in 2024 and 2.3% in 2025.

International food and fuel prices moderating

- The price of Brent crude oil averaged $83.15 per barrel in Q1 2024, down from $84.03 in the previous quarter. The average price is forecast to be $84.00 per barrel in 2024, slightly higher than in 2023. This is nearly $17.00 lower than the 2022 annual average when concerns over the fallout from the Russian invasion of Ukraine saw prices surge. Brent crude oil hit $90.05 per barrel in April 2024 amid escalating tensions in the Middle East, attacks on Russian refineries, and an extension of output cuts through June.

- The World Bank food price index declined in Q1 2024 by 3.9% from the previous quarter. Grain prices were 4.3% lower in Q1 2024 compared to Q4 2023 as wheat and corn prices fell. After the Russian Federation terminated the Black Sea Grain Initiative in July 2023, Ukraine initiated the movement of civilian vessels through a new corridor in October 2023. Establishing this new corridor to resume Black Sea exports has boosted Ukraine's exports of grains and agricultural products, especially corn. Prices of oils and meals also decreased by 5.2% in Q1 2024. On the other hand, rice prices have been continuously rising since the end of 2022, increasing by 3.5% in the same quarter. They will remain high in 2024, assuming India maintains its export restrictions and there will be a moderate-to-strong El Niño.

- Liquefied natural gas (LNG) prices reached record highs in 2022 but have declined continuously since Q2 2023, despite global LNG production remaining relatively tight in 2023. The decline in LNG prices has contributed to increased gas consumption. On the other hand, gold prices continued their upward trajectory, supported by strong demand amid heightened geopolitical tensions. Recent price increases have been supported by strong demand from several emerging markets and developing economies and increased activity in exchange-traded funds in the PRC. Higher prices were also observed for cocoa (43.6%), coffee (4.8%), and coconut oil (9.8%), while prices declined for logs (0.5%) and sugar (4.9%) in Q1 2024.

Tourism in the Pacific shows varying recovery trends

- Australia and New Zealand remain significant visitor markets in the Pacific subregion, and Australian visitors to most major South Pacific destinations have exceeded pre-pandemic levels. Between January and April 2024, Australian visitors to Vanuatu were 14.9% higher than the average for the same periods in 2018–2019. Australian visitors to Fiji and Samoa were up by 18.5% and 29.8%, respectively.

- During the same period, 109,989 New Zealanders visited the Pacific, a 6.0% increase from the 2018–2019 average. The number of New Zealand visitors to the Cook Islands (25,794) was 7.5% higher than pre-pandemic levels, while visitors to Tonga (9,179) were 93.8% of the 2018–2019 average for the same period.

Tourist Departures for Pacific Destinations
('000 persons, January to April totals)

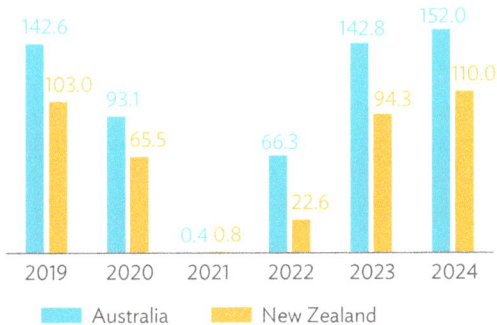

Sources: Government of Australia, Australian Bureau of Statistics. Overseas Arrivals and Departures (accessed 15 June 2024), and Government of New Zealand, Stats NZ Tatauranga Aotearoa: International Travel and Migration (accessed 15 June 2024).

Outbound Tourism from Major Source Markets
(relative to pre–COVID-19 pandemic levels, monthly)

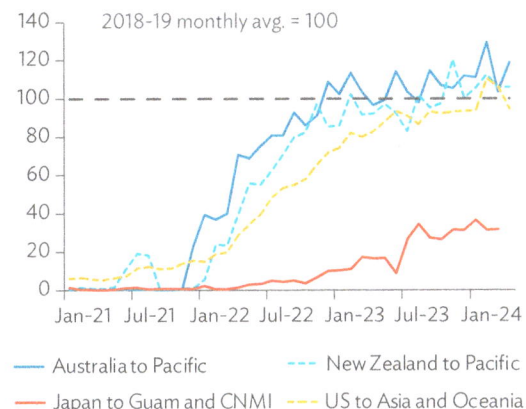

avg. = average, CNMI = Commonwealth of the Northern Mariana Islands, COVID-19 = coronavirus disease, US = United States.

Sources: Government of Australia, Australian Bureau of Statistics. Overseas Arrivals and Departures (accessed 30 June 2024); Government of New Zealand, Stats NZ Tatauranga Aotearoa. International Travel and Migration (accessed 30 June 2024); Government of the US, Department of Commerce International Trade Administration. US Outbound Travel to World Regions (accessed 04 July 2023); and Japan Tourism Marketing Co. Japanese Outbound Tourists Statistics (accessed 30 June 2024).

Lead authors: Ana Isabel Jimenez, Cara Tinio, and Jennifer Umlas.

- In Q1 2024, Tonga welcomed 18,773 visitors, equivalent to 74.9% of the average for the same period in 2018–2019. On the other hand, the total number of visitors to the Cook Islands and Samoa was up by 5.6% and 1.1%, respectively.

- From January to April 2024, Fiji recorded 271,683 visitors. Palau received 19,159 visitors during the same period, equivalent to 48.7% of the average for January–April 2018–2019. Of the total visitors to Palau, most were from the PRC (6,564; or 34.2%), followed by Canada and the US (3,703; 19.3%), and Taipei,China (3,460; 18.1%).

- Air Niugini suspended weekly service from Brisbane, Australia, to Palau via Port Moresby due to low passenger and freight demand. At the same time, Nauru Airlines commenced a nonstop flight between Palau and Brisbane under an Australian-supported scheme. United Airlines, Cambodia Airways, and a major airline based in Taipei,China carried almost 90% of arrivals to Palau in April 2024.

- Air Vanuatu—a state-owned national airline—went into liquidation in May 2024. The airline previously operated flights to Sydney and Brisbane, Australia; Nadi, Fiji; Auckland, New Zealand; and other South Pacific destinations and controlled all the domestic routes. The potential decline in tourism is expected to significantly impact the services sector, including retail and wholesale trade, hospitality, and transport. Moreover, the disruption in air travel in an archipelagic and small state like Vanuatu could limit the availability and mobility of labor and cargo for infrastructure investment (see page 25).

References

Asian Development Bank. 2024. *Asian Development Outlook April 2024.*

Consensus Economics. 2024. *Asia Pacific Consensus Forecasts May 2024.*

Government of Australia, Australian Bureau of Statistics. 2024. Australian National Accounts: National Income, Expenditure and Product. *Media release.* 5 June.

Government of Japan Cabinet Office, Economic and Social Research Institute. 2024. *Quarterly Estimates of GDP, January–March 2024 (the 2nd preliminary).*

Government of New Zealand, Stats NZ Tatauranga Aotearoa. 2024. Gross domestic product: March 2024 quarter. *Media release.* 20 June.

Government of the United States Bureau of Economic Analysis. 2024. Gross Domestic Product (Second Estimate), Corporate Profits (Preliminary Estimate), First Quarter 2024. May.

L. He. 2024. China's economy expands by a surprisingly strong pace in the first quarter of 2024. *CNN.* 16 April.

International Monetary Fund. 2024. *World Economic Outlook: Steady but Slow: Resilience amid Divergence.* April.

International Monetary Fund. 2024. IMF Staff Completes 2024 Article IV Mission to Vanuatu. 20 June.

RNZ. 2024. Domestic market hit by Air Vanuatu fallout. 13 May.

World Bank. 2024. *Commodity Markets Outlook, May 2024.*

COUNTRY ECONOMIC ISSUES

Building Climate and Disaster Resilience in the South Pacific

Lead authors: Lily-Anne Homasi, Ana Isabel Jimenez, Cara Tinio, and Jennifer Umlas

The South Pacific economies of the Cook Islands, Samoa, and Tonga are highly vulnerable to the adverse effects of climate change, including increased intensity of rainfall and tropical storms, rising sea levels, and droughts; disasters triggered by natural hazard including earthquakes, volcanic eruptions, and tsunamis; and health emergencies. This exposure is not just due to geographical location and topography, but also to economic and public finance constraints—including dependence on climate-sensitive sectors such as agriculture, fisheries, and tourism—that can affect the capacity for reconstruction and rehabilitation. With increasing temperatures, shifting rainfall patterns, and rising sea levels, climate change raises disaster risks from flash floods, cyclones, coastal inundation, drought, and vector-borne disease. It also increases the impact of such events, which range from damage to infrastructure, crops, and buildings to the loss of lives and livelihoods.

The World Economic Forum (2023) estimates that global climate change will cost $1.70 trillion to $3.71 trillion by 2050, or $16.00 million per hour. This estimate includes the damage to infrastructure, agriculture, and human health. In the South Pacific, these costs could be 90%–100% of the annual budget, given the crosscutting nature of climate change with adaptation and mitigation activities channeled through sectors such as education, health, transport, and energy. These excessive costs suggest the importance of strategically devising foundational policies that will build the resilience of interventions and their impact on the sustainability of this subregion. Policy areas covering economic governance, as well as social and environmental management, are critical.

COOK ISLANDS

The Cook Islands comprises 15 small islands and is divided into two groups: the northern group being low-lying atolls, and the southern group composed of volcanic islands with low-lying coastal areas and shallow lagoons. The country's topography and remoteness make it highly vulnerable to the impacts of climate change. Disasters include weather extremes such as cyclones and coastal flooding, excessive rainfall, landslides, and droughts, all exacerbated by climate change and sea level rise. The impact of disaster events on gross domestic product (GDP) can be staggeringly high, offsetting development gains. In 2010, Tropical Cyclone Pat affected 12% of the country's total population (78% of the population on the affected island) and required recovery costs equivalent to 3% of GDP (Figure 1). The Pacific Catastrophe Risk Assessment and Financing Initiative indicates that average annual losses from tropical cyclones, earthquakes, and

tsunamis are equivalent to 2% of GDP in the Cook Islands. Probable maximum losses for an event occurring once in 50 years are estimated at $56.8 million for the Cook Islands (PCRAFI; ADB 2024c).

Figure 1: Cook Islands Growth and Fiscal Outcomes

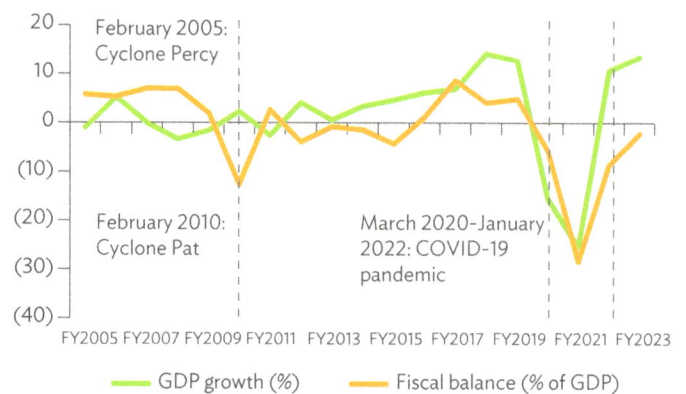

( ) = negative, COVID-19 = coronavirus disease, FY = fiscal year, GDP = gross domestic product.

Note: The fiscal year of the Government of the Cook Islands ends on 30 June.

Sources: Asian Development Bank. *Asian Development Outlook* database (accessed June 2024); and Centre for Research on the Epidemiology of Disasters. The International Disaster Database (accessed July 2024).

Border closures arising from the coronavirus disease (COVID-19) pandemic caused the Cook Islands' tourism-dependent economy to contract by 15.7% in fiscal year (FY) 2020 (ended 30 June 2020 for all three economies discussed in this write-up) and 25.5% in FY2021, the largest contractions in the Pacific subregion during the period. Strategies to grow the economy and build people's resilience to climate change and disasters have been at the forefront of the Cook Islands development agenda.

To mitigate these risks and strengthen the resilience of the Cook Islands to climate change, the government—with support from its development partners—spearheaded policy initiatives in the following areas:

(i) **Establish a legal framework to guide climate change interventions.** In line with Te Kaveiga Nui—National Sustainable Development Plan—and the Cook Islands Economic Development Strategy, the government drafted its first National Cook Islands Climate Change Response Bill. The bill builds on the Climate Change Policy 2018–2028, providing a consolidated approach to reducing national vulnerability and building climate change resilience. The framework and policy documents facilitated the governance and institutional arrangements for climate change initiatives. With support from the Crown Counsel, the Office of the Prime Minister leads the policy side; the Ministry of Finance and Economic Management leads the coordination of public investment; and Infrastructure Cook Islands and the National Environment Services oversee infrastructure projects and safeguard due diligence. The Cook Islands also prepared disease-specific response and recovery plans, such as the *Emergency Response Plan in Cook Islands.*

(ii) **Establish a Sovereign Wealth Fund (SWF).** Lessons from the COVID-19 pandemic underscored the importance for the Cook Islands to build financial assets to mitigate external shocks. This calls for multiple sources of income and the creation of buffers to sustain Cook Islands operations and the well-being of the people during times of crisis. Prior to COVID-19, the Cook Islands had a stabilization fund worth about NZ$50 million (equivalent to 2 months of government operations). This was exhausted during the pandemic, and with the recovery of the economy, it has slowly been built back up. As of 1 July 2024, the balance was equivalent to 3 months' worth of operations. To withstand any future external shocks, the government is establishing the nation's first SWF. Unlike its stabilization fund, the SWF would enable the government to build this financial asset not only from tax receipts, but also gains from fishing licenses, seabed mining, and contributions from development partners and other sources, to directly support its aspirations and build up the amount to provide a safety net for the Cook Islands. This initiative draws on the experiences of other island nation funds, mainly Kiribati, Nauru, and Tuvalu.

(iii) **Invest in critical infrastructure.** Aside from tourism, infrastructure drives economic growth in the Cook Islands. The Cook Islands National Infrastructure Investment Infrastructure Plan (2021) provides the framework and prioritization plan for infrastructure investments. Given the capacity constraints, infrastructure projects on water and sanitation, energy, and health will serve not only the domestic economy but also the critical tourism sector.

(iv) **Support Public Financial Management (PFM) reforms.** The government has also spearheaded several PFM reforms, including digitalizing its tax administration functions and strengthening its medium-term fiscal planning and debt management, as well as procurement and financial management, which are critical for facilitating service delivery. These reforms remain crucial and ongoing development partners' financial and technical advice will ensure they align with international best practices. Digitizing these reforms will sustain government operations during disasters.

(v) **Build an agile public service.** The island nation has an acute labor shortage issue. Cook Islanders are New Zealand passport holders. Hence, the tendency to move to New Zealand and Australia for work is common and can impede the government's ability to deliver services to the public. In recognition of this, the government (with support from development partners) conducted a functional review in 2023. The review emphasized the need to realign similar functions to reduce duplication and support efficiency in government services to the public—for instance, merging climate-related functions and legal and information and communication technology services. This exercise will position the Cook Islands' public workforce to meet current and future challenges and emergencies.

SAMOA

Disasters and health emergencies have had a significant impact on the Samoan economy. Tropical Cyclone Evan in December 2012 caused losses equivalent to 28% of Samoa's GDP ($211 million) and a 2.3% contraction in FY2013 (ADB 2023a). A measles outbreak in late 2019 caused early border closures that halted tourism activity and—together with the onset of the COVID-19 pandemic—drove a 3.1% contraction in GDP in FY2020. The economy shrank by 7.1% in FY2021 and 5.3% in FY2022, as borders remained closed during the pandemic (Figure 2). Although economic growth has since resumed, its sustainability is precarious. The Pacific Catastrophe Risk Assessment and Financing Initiative estimates Samoa's annual average loss from disasters to be equivalent to 1.7% of GDP. However, this may go as high as 5.0% under moderate and extreme climate change scenarios (PCRAFI; ADB 2023a).

Figure 2: Samoa Growth and Fiscal Outcomes

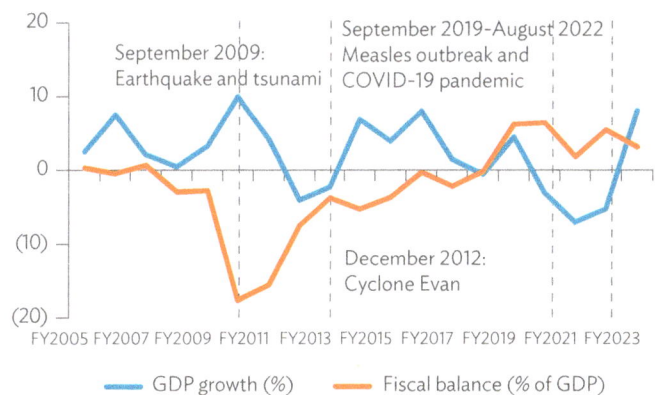

( ) = negative, COVID-19 = coronavirus disease, FY = fiscal year, GDP = gross domestic product.

Note: The fiscal year of the Government of Samoa ends on 30 June.

Sources: Asian Development Bank. *Asian Development Outlook* database (accessed June 2024); and Centre for Research on the Epidemiology of Disasters. The International Disaster Database (accessed July 2024).

Samoa's national development strategies emphasize enhanced climate and disaster resilience. The Pathway for the Development of Samoa FY2021/22–FY2025/26 includes resilience as a crosscutting priority for all sectors, and one of its five key strategic outcomes centers on the environment and climate resilience. The government—supported by development partners—is pursuing investments and reforms in the following areas:

(i) **Infrastructure improvements.** These include expansion in capacity and enhancement of the safety and climate- and disaster-resilience of Apia port, Samoa's sole international maritime gateway. Besides repairing damaged areas and introducing wave monitoring and early warning systems, the project is upgrading the port's breakwater to withstand more severe climate events and developing a plan to guide port operations following a disaster. Other improvements to the Apia port include a new container X-ray scanner that will help enhance border security and facilitate trade. Further, a recently approved Asian Development Bank (ADB) project will construct a multipurpose dam to help mitigate flooding in Apia in extreme rainfall, improve the stability and quality of water supply, and supplement hydropower generation capacity. The project will also support capacity building on flood management and biodiversity conservation.

(ii) **PFM reforms.** Under its Disaster Risk Financing Policy 2022–2025, the Government of Samoa is working to integrate climate and disaster risk analysis into the national budget and planning processes, and exploring options to transfer disaster risk to the private sector, among others (ADB 2023a). It has also established new budget lines for emergency management, which would channel resources to key agencies in times of need.

(iii) **Enhanced social resilience.** In 2023, the government launched the National Social Protection Policy Framework to consolidate existing social protection programs—which cover vulnerable groups comprising women, children, older people, people with disabilities, and those affected by disasters—and ensure that these complement each other and improve their targeting.

TONGA

From 2017–2021, Tonga consistently ranked in the top three on the World Risk Index, which measures countries most at risk from extreme natural events and the adverse impacts of climate change.[1] In FY2018, Cyclone Gita caused losses equivalent to 38.0% of GDP ($157 million), and Tonga's economy contracted by 2.2% in FY2022 primarily due to the January 2022 Hunga Tonga-Hunga Ha'apai (HTHH) volcano eruption and subsequent tsunami and community transmission of COVID-19 (Figure 3). The HTHH eruption and tsunami affected up to 80.0% of the population and caused total damage and loss estimated to be equivalent to 36.4% of GDP (International Federation of Red Cross and Red Crescent Societies 2024, ADB 2023b). Besides causing significant damage to the agricultural sector, it destroyed tourism facilities and limited the tourism sector's ability to contribute to economic recovery after borders were reopened in August 2022. Some of these facilities had just been rebuilt after being damaged by Cyclone Harold in 2020 before being destroyed again by the HTHH event (Webb 2023).

The combined impact of the HTHH volcanic eruption and the COVID-19 pandemic significantly strained the government's limited resources, further emphasizing the need for PFM reforms. Tonga collects only about half of its potential consumption tax revenue due to high levels of noncompliance. A review of tax exemptions is also needed. Based on data from FY2017–FY2022, the Government of Tonga estimated that overall tax revenue losses average T$58 million per annum, equivalent to 7.8% of overall revenue projected for FY2024 (Government of Tonga 2023). Despite improvements in

PFM, several vulnerabilities persist, including weak medium-term budgeting, the absence of a debt management strategy, inadequate legal frameworks for internal audit functions and controls, and a lack of publication requirements for budget documents.

Figure 3: Tonga Growth and Fiscal Outcomes

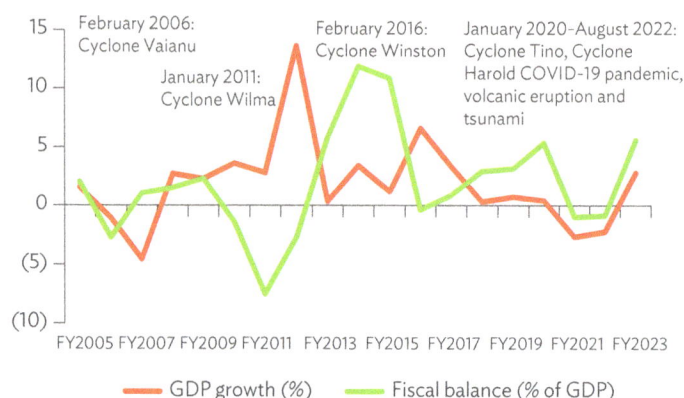

( ) = negative, COVID-19 = coronavirus disease, FY = fiscal year, GDP = gross domestic product, HTHH = Hunga Tonga-Hunga Ha'apai.

Note: The fiscal year of the Government of Tonga ends on 30 June.

Sources: Asian Development Bank. *Asian Development Outlook* database (accessed June 2024); and Centre for Research on the Epidemiology of Disasters. The International Disaster Database (accessed July 2024).

The second Tonga Strategic Development Framework, 2015–2025, sets the vision and provides the framework for Tonga's development. The Economic Institutions pillar focuses on economic growth by creating livelihoods and business opportunities, including improved macroeconomic management and stability, creating a stronger enabling environment for the business sector, and improving access to economic opportunities overseas. Meanwhile, the Natural Resources and Environment Inputs pillar emphasizes "inclusive and sustainable access to well-maintained and protected resources", including improved resilience to extreme weather events and the impact of climate change.

Tonga's policy actions and investments to build resilience include the following:

(i) **Infrastructure improvements.** With over 98% of Tonga's imports arriving by sea, the Nuku'alofa Port is a major doorway to transport and trade. However, it faces inefficiencies due to limited capacity to accommodate larger vessels, low-lying container yards, and poor road connectivity. With the support of development partners—including ADB and the Government of Australia—key upgrades are underway, including expanding the Queen Salote International Wharf to accommodate larger vessels, implementing smart and green port features, and capacity-building to enhance operations. These improvements will enable the port to handle port traffic up to 2040. Nuku'alofa's electricity supply network is also being upgraded. By converting its open overhead network to covered-area bundled conductors, replacing overhead consumer connections with underground cables, shifting to climate-resilient high-standard distribution poles, and replacing aging distribution switchgear, the network's reliability and resilience to extreme weather events should be enhanced. (See page 36 for a case study on climate-resilient power infrastructure in Tonga.)

(ii) **PFM reforms.** Supported by a policy-based grant agreement with ADB, the Government of Tonga continues to pursue improvements to PFM and sustainability. These include the Public Financial Management Bill, which codifies fiscal responsibility principles and requires the preparation of a medium-term fiscal strategy, establishes an internal audit function, sets a numerical limit on new debt, and provides guidance and deadlines for the online publication of budget documents, among others; and the ongoing implementation of the Electronic Sales Register System, which transmits point-of-sale transaction data to assist in assessing tax liability, evaluating risk, strengthening enforcement of consumption tax, and partially automating value-added tax returns. Retail providers are migrating to the new system, and all the target traders for Phase 1 were onboarded (Government of Tonga 2023).

(iii) **Enhanced social resilience.** The COVID-19 pandemic exposed gaps in social protection programs, prompting the need to develop disaster management plans to ensure responsive and efficient assistance after disasters. Tonga's National Social Protection Policy consolidates social protection programs under an umbrella framework. It also reviews existing social protection programs; identifies gaps; and outlines the country's vision, mission, policy principles, and priorities for the next decade.

(iv) **Improving trade stability.** The Authorized Economic Operator Secure Export Scheme is a pilot program implemented to improve private sector resilience in the face of trade disruptions. The scheme establishes a network of accredited and vetted suppliers and transporters and streamlines export processes to reduce transaction costs and time to export, which is especially beneficial for perishable goods.

CONCLUSION AND RECOMMENDATIONS

The small island developing states of the South Pacific face various challenges due to their remote locations, small and narrow economic bases, and high vulnerability to shocks. These factors contribute to higher production and public service delivery costs and help limit institutional capacity development and private sector growth. The increased frequency and intensity of extreme climatic and weather events and the ever-present risk of external shocks highlight the importance of reforms to strengthen resilience while improving fiscal sustainability and fostering inclusive growth.

South Pacific governments are pursuing measures on multiple fronts to bolster resilience. Programmatic approaches are necessary to prioritize and coordinate multiple activities and resources in the same policy area; for instance, risk assessments can inform infrastructure investment programming and gender-responsive policy frameworks (see page 42 for a discussion on ADB's fragility

risk assessments). These can also help identify and estimate the fiscal and economic risks from disasters and other likely shocks, which could then guide annual budgeting and financing-related discussions with development partners. Finally, proper targeting of interventions such as social protection measures—for example, through establishing a database of eligible recipients—should maximize the efficient use of resources.

Note

[1]   In 2022, the methodology for calculating the World Risk Index was revised to include absolute numbers and percentage figures of the countries' at-risk populations, among other changes. The rankings of many Pacific economies changed substantially as a result.

References

Asian Development Bank (ADB). 2019. Samoa: Enhancing Safety, Security, and Sustainability of Apia Port Project.

ADB. 2023a. Pacific Disaster Resilience Program (Phase 4).

ADB. 2023b. Kingdom of Tonga: Improving Economic Management Program, Subprogram 1.

ADB. 2024a. ADB Signs $10 Million Grant to Help Tonga's Economic Recovery After Disasters and Health Emergencies. News release. 12 April.

ADB. 2024b. Samoa: Alaoa Multipurpose Dam Project.

ADB. 2024c. Pacific Disaster Resilience Program (Phase 5).

Bündnis Entwicklung Hilft. *WorldRiskReport* (6 years: 2017–2022).

Government of the Cook Islands. 2021. *Cook Islands Infrastructure Investment Plan.*

Government of the Cook Islands. 2024. *2024–2025 National Budget.*

Government of the Kingdom of Tonga, Ministry of Revenue and Customs. 2023. *Annual Report Financial Year 2022/2023.*

Government of the Kingdom of Tonga, Ministry of Finance. 2023. *Budget statement for the year ending 30 June 2024.*

International Federation of Red Cross and Red Crescent Societies. 2024. *Hunga Tonga Hunga Ha'apai - Emergency appeal №: MDRTO002 Final Report.*

Pacific Catastrophe Risk Assessment and Financing Initiative. Country Risk Profiles (accessed June 2024).

J. Webb. 2023. Rebuilding and rehiring: An update on post-COVID-19 tourism in Samoa and Tonga. *Pacific Economic Monitor.* July.

World Economic Forum. 2023. *Climate Change is costing the world $16 million per hour: study.*

Fiji's New Budget: Walking the Tightrope

Lead authors: Isoa Wainiqolo and Jennifer Umlas

Following the COVID-19 pandemic, Fiji's economy experienced a notable resurgence, primarily attributed to the return of tourists, resulting in a 7.8% increase in GDP in 2023. The recovery of the tourism sector has reduced the current account deficit to 9.5% of GDP. Further strengthening the economic landscape, foreign exchange reserves now provide coverage for approximately 5.2 months of potential imports. Concurrently, the fiscal deficit decreased from 12.1% of GDP in FY2022 (ending 31 July 2022) to 7.1% in FY2023.

Despite these signs of recovery, supply-side challenges in tourism-related sectors are poised to impact the short-term economic outlook. Public debt declined from 90.6% of GDP at the end of FY2022 to 78.0% at the end of FY2024. However, it remains high relative to a pre-pandemic level of 48.8% at the end of FY2019, constraining the government's capacity to expand productive investments. The combination of a slowdown in tourist arrivals, underperforming resource-based sectors, reduced domestic consumption due to high emigration rates, and delays in investment projects may exert downward pressure on Fiji's short- to medium-term growth prospects. Consequently, the projected GDP growth is 3.0% for 2024 and 2.7% for 2025.

The Parliament of Fiji passed the FY2025 national budget on 11 July 2024. It must navigate carefully to keep its debt targets on track while maintaining economic growth. However, given limited resources, empowering the private sector to drive economic growth and ease the strain on government finances is equally important.

PAST YEAR'S BUDGET PERFORMANCE

Guided by its medium-term fiscal strategy for FY2024 to FY2026, the government budgeted to reduce the fiscal deficit from 7.1% of GDP in FY2023 to 4.8% of GDP in FY2024. It has taken major steps to reverse lost revenues from tax policy changes and the economic downturn during the COVID-19 period. The International Monetary Fund (IMF) estimated that Fiji lost revenue equivalent to 5.0% of GDP due to the extensive tax cuts in the FY2021 budget (IMF 2021).

In the FY2024 budget, the VAT rate was increased from 9.0% to 15.0%, and the corporate tax rate from 20.0% to 25.0%. VAT represents about 40.0% of total government revenue. As a tourist-dependent economy, VAT captures revenues from tourism and reduces reliance on other forms of taxes.

While the government anticipated that over 83.0% of its revenue in FY2024 would come from taxes, actual tax revenue is expected to be 2.3% lower than the budget projection. Contrary to expectations, VAT collections slowed toward the end of the fiscal year. The government attributed this to weak compliance and slow consumer spending due to increased emigration. However, corporate and personal income tax collection was higher than budgeted (Figure 4).

Figure 4: Fiji Budget Performance (FY2023–FY2024)

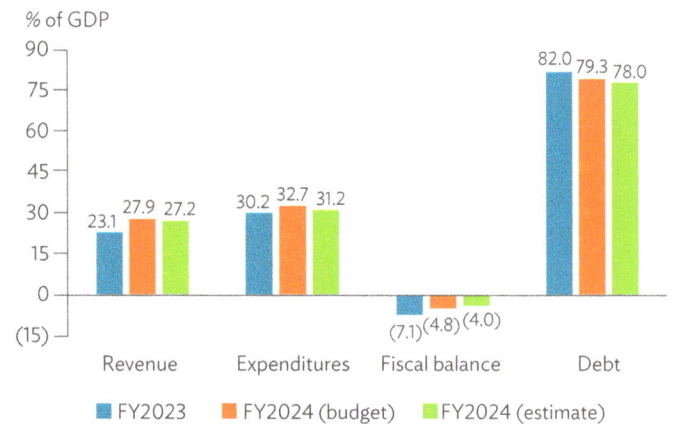

( ) = negative, FY = fiscal year, GDP = gross domestic product.
Note: The fiscal year of the Government of Fiji ends on 31 July.
Source: Government of Fiji. *Budget Supplement FY2024–2025.*

Expenditure in FY2024 was 5.4% below target, partly due to human and physical capital constraints. Increasing emigration and those opting for private-sector opportunities adversely affected the government's human resource capacity. The lack of project readiness likely delayed some capital projects.

NEW BUDGET HIGHLIGHTS

The government has initiated a New Development Plan (NDP) 2025–2029 to stimulate the economy and attain a more inclusive and sustainable growth trajectory. The NDP centers on three key pillars: bolstering economic resilience, empowering citizens, and ensuring sound governance. These pillars are well-aligned with the FY2025 budget. For instance, the government has earmarked F$2.7 million to implement a new budget system.

The new budget has sought to rejuvenate the health systems, specifically focusing on primary health care. This together with measures aimed at strengthening social protection programs, additional funding for public works and road infrastructure, and rationalization of the tax system are all expected to lay the foundation for more resilient and inclusive growth and to contribute to realizing the objectives of the NDP.

The budget has also been integrated into the Medium Term Fiscal Strategy FY2024–2027, with the overarching objective of upholding macroeconomic stability and attaining sustainable and resilient growth. The strategy also emphasizes gender-responsive budgeting through targeted allocations and policies. To sustain the public debt-to-GDP ratio at viable levels, the government's medium-term debt strategy will focus on (i) minimizing the medium- to long-term cost of government debt within prudent risk levels and (ii) fostering the development of a well-functioning domestic market for debt securities. Subsequently, the government's 15-year Fiscal Framework FY2024–2025 to FY2039–2040 targets economic growth of 3.0% and an inflation rate of 2.0%–3.0%, with the resulting public debt-to-GDP ratio expected to decrease from 77.8% at the end of FY2025 to 60.0% by FY2040. Figure 6 provides a snapshot of the government's medium-term fiscal framework.

Figure 5: Fiji Major Government Spending for FY2010– FY2025

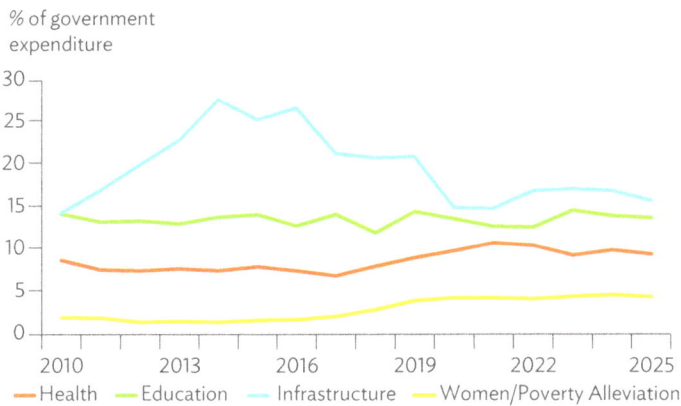

% of government expenditure

Health   Education   Infrastructure   Women/Poverty Alleviation

FY = fiscal year.
Note: The fiscal year of the Government of Fiji ends on 31 July.
Source: Government of Fiji. Ministry of Finance Various Budget Estimates.

In its FY2025 budget, the government projects revenue to increase by 9.5% and the tax-to-GDP ratio to increase to 23.5% from 23.1% in FY2024. Without major revenue policy changes or grant funding, the government depends on improved collections, sustained general improvement in demand, and widening the tax base.

Total expenditure in FY2025 is budgeted at F$4.55 billion, or 10.9% higher than the revised estimate for FY2024. The government is planning a 15.0% increase in personnel costs to accommodate salary increments and superannuation contributions. Salary-based civil servants will receive a 7.0%-10.0% pay rise, while wage earners will get a 10.0%-20.0% increment. The government remains firmly committed to investment in education, with 13.8% of expenditure allocated to the Ministry of Education for continuing programs such as free primary and secondary education, back-to-school support, transport assistance, and tertiary scholarship and new cost-sharing scholarship initiatives with overseas universities.

The government also aims to fast-track the corporatization of the Water Authority of Fiji (WAF). Key challenges in the water sector include climate change impacts, aging infrastructure, growing demand from a rapidly growing tourism sector, skills shortages, and an unviable financial model. Fiji charges one of the lowest residential water rates in the Pacific at F$0.15 per 1,000 megaliters, covering less than half of the supply's operational cost. WAF loses about 47.0% of clean water due to aging infrastructure, needing F$3 billion to replace. Despite the government allocating 5.7% of its expenditure to WAF over the last four budgets, significant cost savings could be achieved with a new tariff structure that reflects actual operation costs. However, this needs to be complemented by relevant subsidies that protect low-income households.

Figure 6: Fiji Medium-Term Fiscal Framework

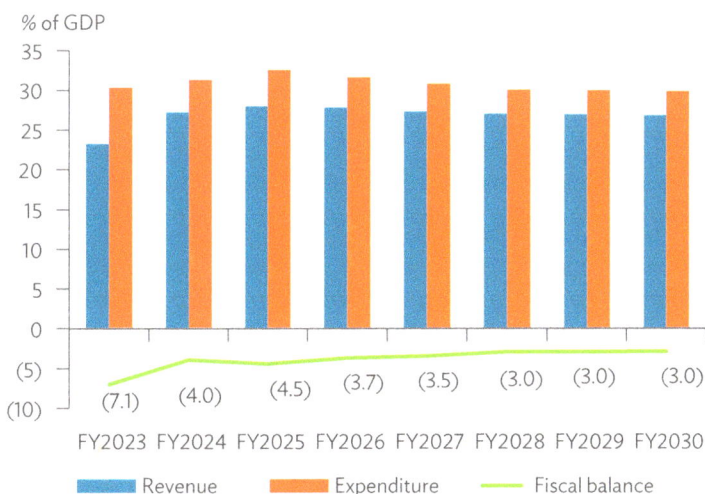

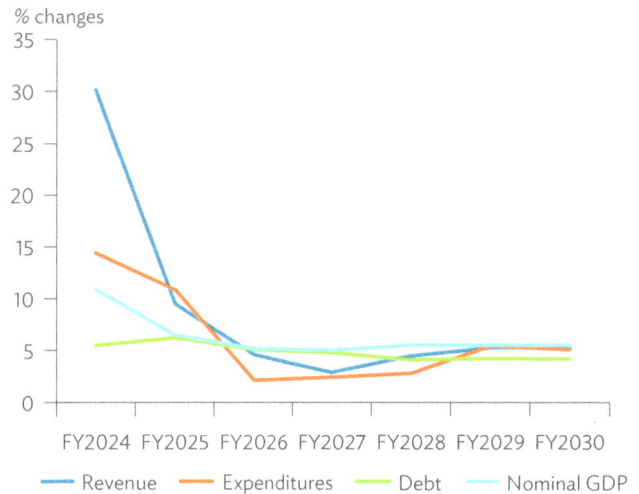

( ) = negative, FY = fiscal year, GDP = gross domestic product.
Note: The fiscal year of the Government of Fiji ends on 31 July.
Source: ADB staff computation based on the Government of Fiji. *Budget Supplement FY2024–2025*.

IMPENDING RISKS

The new budget identifies macroeconomic risks as the most significant threat to its fiscal consolidation efforts. The budget relies on continued improving demand to boost revenue collections and GDP growth to reduce the debt-to-GDP ratio.

Two scenarios were considered to demonstrate this. Under the baseline scenario, the government's current fiscal consolidation path is detailed in its FY2025 budget, which includes a gradual reduction in the fiscal deficit-to-GDP ratio from 4.5% in FY2025 to 3.0% by FY2030. The alternative scenario introduced a 3.0% negative nominal GDP shock in FY2025. This simulation demonstrates that, at a minimum, any macroeconomic shock leading to a decline in GDP will delay its fiscal consolidation path (Figure 7).

Figure 7: Fiji Government Scenarios Under Macroeconomic Shocks

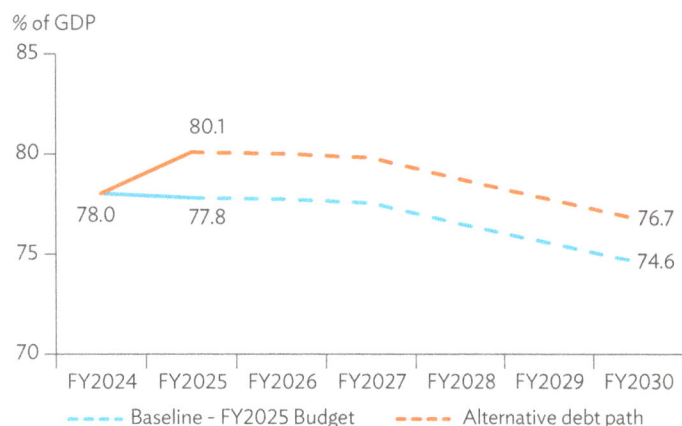

FY = fiscal year, GDP = gross domestic product.
Note: The fiscal year of the Government of Fiji ends on 31 July.
Source: ADB staff computation based on the Government of Fiji. *Budget Supplement FY2024–2025.*

In its 2024 Article IV report, the IMF recommended a combination of revenue and expenditure measures to further support Fiji's fiscal consolidation. Key revenue suggestions included reducing exemptions and incentives, simplifying the personal income tax structure, introducing a dividend tax, and unifying VAT rates while better targeting vulnerable people. The IMF advised improving spending efficiency, especially on transfers, supplies, consumables, and right-sizing the public sector. For capital investment, the report emphasized enhancing public investment management, project planning, prioritization, costings, and monitoring. The IMF estimated that these reforms could generate at least 3.5% of GDP in additional revenues and cost savings, lowering the debt-to-GDP ratio to below 67.0% by FY2029.

INVESTMENT

Investment fosters development by creating employment opportunities and stimulating economic activities. In Fiji, capital investment holds significant importance owing to prevailing infrastructure deficiencies. The government has established the Investment Facilitation Committee with the primary objective of addressing persistent or unresolved impediments to investment and business activities and implementing regulatory reforms to enhance the business environment and foster investment growth. The businessNOW portal system provides entrepreneurs and investors with a streamlined platform to lodge and monitor their applications across diverse government agencies.

Based on the National Development Plan, the government has maintained a target for investment at approximately 25.0% of GDP.[1] However, from 2010 to 2022, investment levels fluctuated, averaging 20.6% of GDP and peaking at 27.6% in 2013 (Figure 8).

Figure 8: Fiji Investment Trend

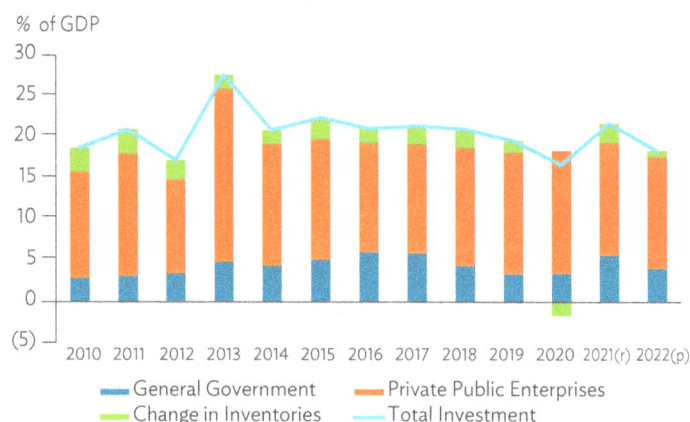

( ) = negative, FY = fiscal year, GDP = gross domestic product, p = provisional, r = revised.
Note: The fiscal year of the Government of Fiji ends on 31 July.
Source: Government of Fiji, Reserve Bank of Fiji. 2024. Investments 1980–2022

Foreign direct investment (FDI) has generally remained low and static since 2010. Net FDI averaged 6.4% of GDP during 2010–2022, peaking at 9.5% of GDP in 2021. FDI inflows have been unpredictable and focused on specific industries, particularly high-end tourism.

Infrastructure and economic development investment can effectively broaden the tax base, increasing revenue collection. The additional tax revenue could bolster public programs, enhance service delivery, or mitigate existing debt burdens.

WAY FORWARD

To sustain robust economic growth and enhance economic resilience, the government must concentrate on improving expenditure efficiency, enhancing budget execution, and advancing major private investment projects. This includes streamlining immigration and business application processes, which are crucial in boosting new economic activities and facilitating the private sector's increase in hotel capacity.

While the current emphasis on fiscal consolidation is necessary to reverse the trend of public debt, strengthening fiscal buffers and maintaining macroeconomic stability are equally critical due to Fiji's susceptibility to economic shocks. The limited fiscal space to absorb potential future disturbances remains a cause for concern, highlighting the need for ongoing efforts to improve expenditure efficiency.

Promoting growth-oriented spending and strengthening implementation capacity are paramount for fostering resilient and inclusive growth while reducing debt levels. Given the pivotal role of state-owned enterprises in the economy, measures such as broadening regulatory and governance standards, enhancing their capabilities, and establishing a framework to limit state-owned enterprise guarantees can create additional fiscal leeway for productive investments.

Ultimately, the focus should be on fiscal sustainability and prioritizing resources to support societal needs and infrastructure for inclusive and sustainable growth. The government may need to bolster implementation capacity to address the under-execution of capital spending. To achieve these objectives, the new budget and the Medium Term Fiscal Strategy provide fiscal targets to promote macroeconomic stability and achieve resilient growth.

Note

[1] 5-Year and 20-Year National Development Plan.

References

Government of Fiji, Ministry of Finance, Strategic Planning, National Development and Statistics. 2023. *Medium Term Fiscal Strategy 2024–2026*. Parliamentary Paper No. 7 of 2023.

Government of Fiji, Ministry of Finance, Strategic Planning, National Development and Statistics. 2023c. *Budget Supplement 2024–2025*.

International Monetary Fund (IMF). 2021. Republic of Fiji 2021 Article IV Consultation. *IMF Country Report*. No. 24/159.

IMF. 2024. Republic of Fiji 2024 Article IV Consultation. *IMF Country Report*. No. 21/157.

Reserve Bank of Fiji (RBF). 2019. Investment and Economic Growth.

Water Authority of Fiji. 2024. Fiji Water Sector Strategy 2050.

High Cost of Living Undermines Social Protection Impact: The Cases of Kiribati, Niue, and Tuvalu

Lead authors: Lily-Anne Homasi, Isoa Wainiqolo, Ana Isabel Jimenez, and Jennifer Umlas

Kiribati, Niue, and Tuvalu are susceptible to extreme weather events, including drought, cyclones, heavy rainfall, and coastal flooding. The combination of high exposure to these disasters and limited capacity for disaster adaptation and mitigation exacerbates their impact on the population. The small size of these economies and high transportation costs make them vulnerable to economic shocks, which can easily strain limited government resources. These factors make response and recovery efforts more challenging.

Kiribati and Tuvalu have managed to bounce back from the economic downturn experienced in 2020, which was supported by the resumption of infrastructure projects and fiscal stimulus, including social protection spending. A copra subsidy and unemployment benefits supported Kiribati household incomes and domestic consumption, while Tuvalu revived economic activity in construction, trade, and hospitality. However, Niue's economy is still struggling to recover, with visitor arrivals remaining below pre-pandemic levels. Post-pandemic, the three economies face the challenge of high living costs due to a surge in inflation. The distance of these economies from markets and narrow production bases make them price takers but also increase their susceptibility to high transportation costs.

Kiribati and Tuvalu use the Australian dollar, while Niue uses the New Zealand dollar. From 2019 to 2023, both currencies were relatively stable, with the nominal effective exchange rate depreciating by only 0.4% on average each year against trading partner currencies. According to the IMF, the global commodity price index rose by 35.2%, with fuel and energy price index increasing by 32.4% and food price index by 38.9%.

This write-up will outline the main contributors to inflation by comparing the consumer price index at the end of 2019 and 2023, reviewing social protection support in these economies, and offering policy suggestions for consideration.

HIGH COST OF LIVING

In Kiribati, inflation reached 25.1% year-on-year (y-o-y) in January 2023 due to increased domestic demand, supply shortages, higher global commodity prices, and rising freight costs. Inflation has since been trending down and reached -2.1% y-o-y in December 2023, driven by the moderation of global commodity prices and improved supply-side conditions. However, by comparing the consumer price index at the end of 2019 and 2023, prices increased by about 20%. Food prices increased by about 26%, housing by more than 5%, and transport by more than 8% (Figure 9).

Figure 9: Kiribati – Contributors to Inflation

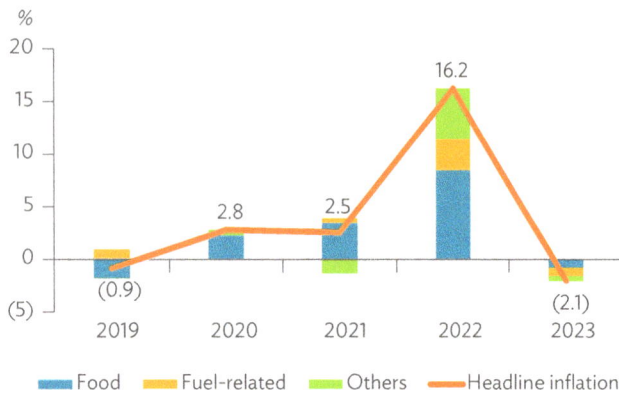

( ) = negative.
Sources: Government of Kiribati, National Statistics Office (accessed 29 July 2024), International Monetary Fund, and ADB estimates.

Figure 11: Tuvalu – Contributors to Inflation

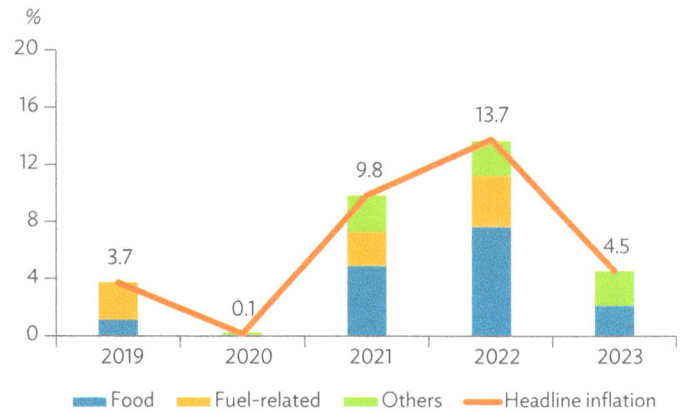

Sources: Government of Tuvalu, International Monetary Fund, and ADB estimates (accessed 01 July 2024).

Movements in food prices explained more than 80% of overall price changes in 2020 and about 52% in 2022. These price movements made it harder for residents and visitors in Kiribati to afford nutritional food.

In Niue, consumer prices increased by about 20% from 2019 to 2023. Compared to 2019, food prices had risen by 28% at the end of 2023. This upward trend is attributed to the escalating prices of sheep and chicken meat. The cost of essential utilities such as housing, water, electricity, and gas also increased. Housing prices surged by 12.5% during 2019–2023, furnishing and household equipment prices by 16.8%, and transport prices by 45.3%.

Figure 10: Niue – Contributors to Inflation

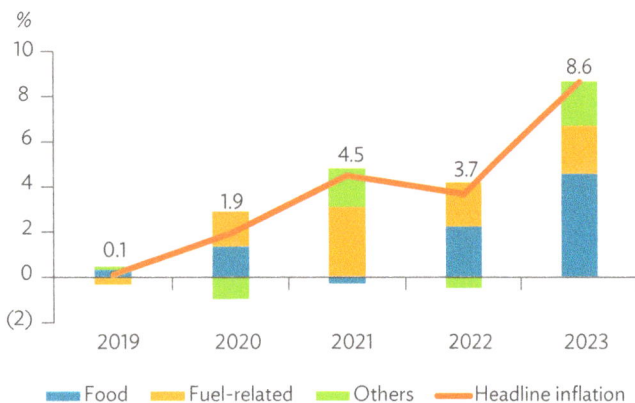

( ) = negative.
Note: Years are fiscal years ending on June of that year.
Sources: ADB estimates and Government of Niue, Statistics Niue (accessed 01 July 2024).

In Tuvalu, consumer prices increased by 31.0% by the end of 2023 compared to 2019. Food prices rose by 42%. Inflation surged during 2019–2023 due to the implementation of sin taxes and high fuel prices resulting from Russia's war in Ukraine and its impact on supply (Figure 11).

From 2021 to 2023, food prices explained more than half of the overall price changes, and fuel-related expenditures more than one-quarter of the price changes from 2021 to 2022.[1]

SOCIAL PROTECTION MEASURES

Social protection programs are generally classified into three categories: social insurance, social assistance, and labor market programs.

In Kiribati, spending on social protection was equivalent to about 8% of GDP before the pandemic. In 2021, almost 58% of the allocation for social protection went to the unemployment benefits program, as border closures resulted in job losses.

The Copra Price Subsidy, Senior Citizens Benefit, School Fee Support for Underprivileged Children, Disability Support Allowance, and more recently, the Unemployment Benefit, make up make up the other formal social protection programs in Kiribati. Although the Kiribati Provident Fund has potential social protection aims, the main cash transfer programs are the Copra Price Subsidy and the Senior Citizens Benefit.

In Niue, social insurance[2] made up 14.3% of total social protection spending in 2018 (latest data available), while social assistance made up 85.6%, which included spending on a pension scheme, child welfare, newborn infant grants, welfare disability benefits, funerals, special assistance, and welfare hardship benefits. The older population (60 years and above)—accounting for 20.0% of the population—takes up 92.0% of total social protection expenditures. School enrollment is free and compulsory for children aged 5–16.

The Government of Niue provides NZ$85 per fortnight per eligible child from birth until 18. There is also a one-off newborn infant/baby incentive grant of NZ$2,000, disbursed in four fortnightly payments. Those with disabilities receive a welfare disability cash transfer of NZ$150–NZ$180 per fortnight until they find full employment.

A welfare hardship benefit of NZ$100–NZ$150 is available to those who meet a specific criterion, such as job loss or time spent as a caregiver.

In Tuvalu, formal social protection is concentrated on the Senior Citizen Scheme, which accounts for 88.0% of government spending. The monthly payment under the Senior Citizen Scheme (70 years old and above) is A$100 per person. Education is free and compulsory for children aged 6–15.

Tuvalu's social protection budget (which includes grants, subsidies, and donations; the medical treatment scheme, scholarship, and training) made up an average of 15.8% of total expenditures in 2018 and 2019. It increased to 26.6% in the 2022 budget and was 21.5% of the 2023 budget. Grants, subsidies, and donations ranged from 5.0% to 7.0% of total expenditures from 2018 to 2020, while the medical scheme averaged 6.0% of spending. The bulk of scholarships are taken up by tertiary education.

POLICY CONSIDERATIONS

High inflation reduces the purchasing power of social welfare in these countries unless grants are increased. However, increasing government support could strain already limited fiscal resources. These small economies rely heavily on imports, and their remote location increases transportation and costs of doing business, thereby limiting their options. Despite this, there may still be potential avenues for governments to support vulnerable households.

(i)   **Targeting social protection programs.** Review and update registries to correctly identify vulnerable groups, assist in evidence-informed decision-making and budgeting, and prevent aid from overlapping.

(ii) **Building financial literacy.** As part of the social protection package, these countries—with the support of development partners and relevant financial institutions—deliver targeted training to ensure recipients of these social welfare programs budget and spend their funds to meet their basic needs.

(iii) **Strengthening price monitoring.** Close price monitoring is crucial so decision-makers are well-informed. If government budgets allow, taxes and duties should be reviewed periodically.

(iv) **Financing energy-efficient appliances.** Kiribati, Niue, and Tuvalu can lower household electricity bills and reduce carbon emissions by using renewable energy and other clean energy devices.

Notes

[1] In Tuvalu, fuel-related expenditures include housing costs (such as cooking gas) and transport costs (such as fuel for daily travel).

[2] Social insurance programs include pensions, insurance, provident funds, unemployment insurance, and worker compensation schemes.

References

Asian Development Bank (ADB). 2022a. *Pacific Economic Monitor.*

ADB. 2022b. *The Social Protection Indicator for the Pacific. Tracking Developments in Social Protection.*

ADB. 2023a. *Asian Development Outlook Central Pacific Economies.*

ADB. 2023b. Regional: Enhancing ADB's Support for Social Protection to Achieve the Sustainable Development Goals Niue: 2018 Social Protection Indicator.

ADB. Nd. Sector Assessment (Summary): Public Sector Management (Disaster Risk Management).

Government of Kiribati, Ministry of Finance and Economic Development. 2022-2024. *National Budget.*

Government of Tuvalu, Ministry of Finance. 2022a. *2023 National Budget.*

Government of Tuvalu, Ministry of Finance. 2022b. Tuvalu Development Partners Collaboration (presentation).

International Monetary Fund (IMF). 2024a. *2024 Article IV Consultation Staff Report – Kiribati.*

IMF. 2024b. *World Economic Outlook Database* (accessed 5 July 2024).

World Bank. 2023. Tuvalu First Climate and Disaster Resilience Development Policy Financing.

Developing a Resilient Labor Market in Nauru

Lead authors: Katherine Passmore and Prince Cruz

Using results from the 2021 Nauru Population and Housing Census, this write-up explores how Nauru is building labor market resilience through investments in education and training, including various programs designed to improve education and labor outcomes.

Nauru faces challenges common to small island states, including a narrow economic base, remote location, small population, and insufficient infrastructure. The major driver of recent economic activity is the Australian-financed Regional Processing Center (RPC)—an immigration detention facility for offshore processing of asylum seekers. However, the RPC has been winding down, and the number of employees fell from 575 at the end of 2021 to 50 a year later. In preparation for its possible closure, the Government of Nauru, in partnership with the Government of Australia, initiated the Alternative Pathways Program (APP) in 2023. This program was designed to train RPC staff and family members affected by the closure for employment opportunities in other sectors of the economy.

THE EDUCATION SYSTEM AND LABOR MARKET

Education in Nauru is mandatory and free. Children must be enrolled until they complete the school year during which they turn 18. School attendance has been an ongoing problem, with estimated attendance rates declining from 54% in 2016 to 44% in 2018 and 40% in 2023.[1] The 2020 Voluntary National Review of the United Nations' Sustainable Development Goals noted that:

> The low attendance rates are perplexing considering that the government has introduced many policies to encourage attendance such as the free lunch program, free transport, the engagement of expatriate teachers, employment of liaison officers for each government school, and the allocation of considerable expenditure to improve school buildings and facilities. In May 2016, the Nauru Education Assistance Trust (NEAT) scheme was introduced as a further encouragement to students to attend school by offering [A]$5 for each day that they attend school, payable after graduation at the end of Year 12. The attendance rates spiked considerably in the early days, but the numbers have since dropped again.[2]

During the COVID-19 pandemic, the government introduced a back-to-school payment of A$50 per child per term. The payment is to ensure students are 'school ready' by covering essential items including uniforms and stationery. Spending for these programs rose to 3.8% of GDP in the 2024 budget from an average of 2.7% in FY2019 to FY2021 (Figure 12).

Figure 12: Nauru Educational Support Schemes

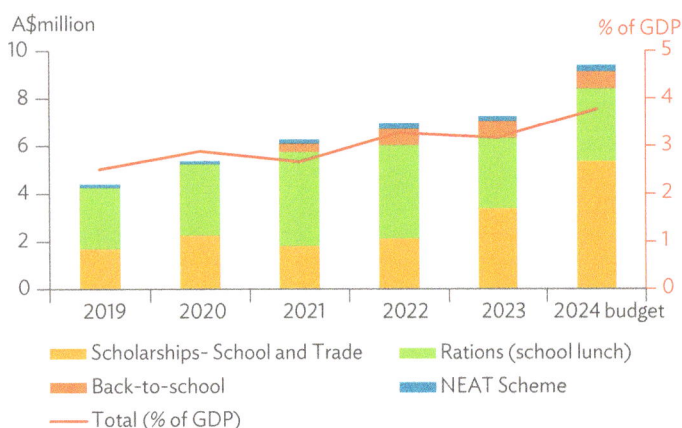

GDP = gross domestic product, NEAT = Nauru Education Assistance Trust.
Note. Years are fiscal years ending June of that year.
Source: ADB estimates using data from Nauru budget documents.

The 2021 Census reported a significantly higher attendance rate, but this was based on parent responses rather than recorded school attendance. Census numbers also indicate that attendance rates were slightly higher for females than males, but there remains a significant gap between primary and secondary school attendance (Figure 13).[3]

Figure 13: Nauru School Attendance Rate, 2021

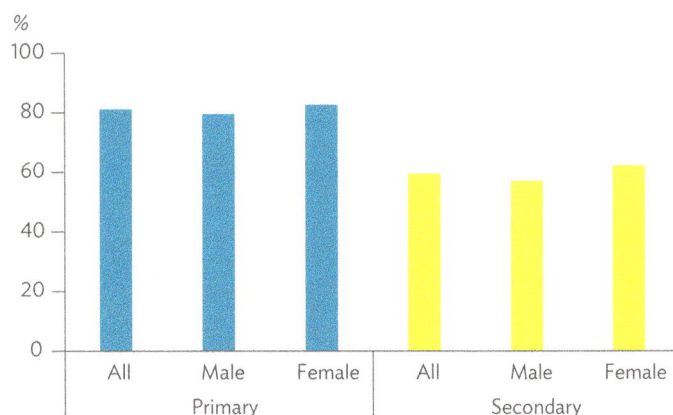

Source: Pacific Community and Government of Nauru. 2023. *Nauru 2021 Population and Housing Census: Analytical Report.*

Comparing 2021 census data with 2011 census data, the proportion of adults (15 years old and above) that had reached at least primary, secondary, or tertiary education appears relatively stable over the decade (Table 1). However, authorities should be mindful of the slight decline in those reaching at least secondary education, with the female attainment rate falling from 92.6% in 2011 to 90.5% in 2021.

Table 1: Nauru Educational Attainment and Literacy Rates, 2011 and 2021
(% of the population)

	2011	2021
Highest grade attained (15 y.o. and above)		
Up to primary education	4.0	4.2
Up to secondary education	91.2	89.2
Male	89.7	88.3
Female	92.6	90.5
Up to tertiary education	4.9	4.2
Adult literacy rate (15 y.o. and above)	96.5	89.6
Male	95.7	86.5
Female	97.2	92.6
Youth literacy rate (15–24 y.o.)	95.6	87.2
Male	94.4	82.8
Female	96.8	91.8

y.o. = years old
Sources: Government of Nauru 2011 and 2021 Censuses.

The government should also address the significant drop in literacy rates. Literacy rates for males were lower than for females, with the gap widening over the decade. The census numbers also obscure declining English literacy. With English as the primary language of instruction and the only mode used by teachers and trainers from Australia and Fiji, many students encounter learning difficulties as both the subject and the mode of instruction (English) appear foreign to them.[4] This highlights the need to train more Nauruan teachers, especially for lower grade levels. The falling English proficiency also limits opportunities for further training or education overseas.

Labor force participation rates for females are consistently lower than for males (Table 2). This reflects that nearly three times more women than men reported caring for the household and family as their primary activity (28% of women and 10% of men). Although the gap between the male and female unemployment rate is insignificant, the rise in youth not in employment, education, or training from 2019 to 2021 is concerning.

Table 2: Nauru Labor Market Indicators, 2011, 2019, and 2021

	2011	2019	2021
Labor force participation rate (%)	64.0	63.0	67.0
Male	78.9	75.0	76.0
Female	49.3	52.0	58.0
Unemployment rate (%)	23.0	18.0	5.0
Male	21.4	18.0	4.9
Female	25.5	19.0	5.2
Youth not in employment, education, or training (%)	...	37.0	40.1
Male	...	30.0	33.4
Female	...	44.0	48.9

... = data not available.
Source: Government of Nauru. 2011 and 2021 Censuses, and 2019 Mini-census.

ALTERNATIVE PATHWAYS PROGRAM

The APP was initially intended for around 800 workers (20% of the labor force) expected to be affected by the RPC downsizing; however, the APP was later offered to the public. The roles filled by Nauruans at the RPC covered key operational areas including security, maintenance, and hospitality. Through the Fiji National University (FNU), the APP provides full qualification and award courses in a range of other fields including construction, training of trainers, welding, automotive, trade testing, hairdressing, culinary arts, nursing, boating, teacher training, and a Bachelor of Science in Fisheries.[5] More than 100 participants graduated from the first session of the APP in 2023. In 2024, 710 participants from the second to sixth sessions of the training programs graduated.[6] Nineteen graduates were identified as eligible for higher level courses, which the government attests demonstrates its commitment to "capacity building the people of Nauru."[7]

Beyond the new skills and knowledge, the APP is founded on "empowerment and resilience" principles. One APP participant noted she could accumulate savings once she learned to sew clothes for herself and her children after graduating from an APP fashion and design course. A different participant who completed

the APP course for office administration moved into an office staff position after working for more than 20 years as a cleaner in the same office. Some participants had years of experience as plumbers, automotive technicians, or electricians but did not have the formal training and certification that the APP could finally give them. This qualification has opened opportunities, including work requiring formal qualifications, further training in Australia or Fiji, and even the chance to become a trainer.

With the APP funded only until 2026, the program's implementers hope it can be extended and expanded. They are exploring collaborating with the local technical and vocational education and training office, the University of the South Pacific, the Australia Pacific Training Coalition, and FNU to provide more training in Nauruan and more course contextualization for the local economy. The success of the APP program will be measured by absorption of graduates into the labor market.

SEASONAL WORKER PROGRAMS AND LINKS TO THE DOMESTIC LABOR MARKET

Nauru has been participating in the Australian and New Zealand seasonal worker programs for many years. While Nauruan participation in these schemes has been relatively low compared to other Pacific nations, the schemes have been expanding. Recent reforms to the Australian programs have resulted in a broader range of opportunities for Nauruans in a wider a range of sectors, including both short-term and long-term opportunities. The New Zealand Recognised Seasonal Employer (RSE) program has also progressively increased the number of RSE places available annually to meet increased employer demand.[8] These schemes provide opportunities for skills development during deployment, which contribute to building resilience in the Nauru labor market as workers return home with more experience and expertise. However, continued investment in the domestic labor market is vital to fill any gaps created by those who leave temporarily to participate in the schemes. A move toward broader recognition of qualifications attained in Nauru will compound skills development and learning opportunities for seasonal workers.

CONCLUSION

The APP has proven to be a popular and empowering program. While the APP initially responded to declining RPC activity, in June 2024 the RPC reverted to "active" mode from "enduring capability" mode.[9] While RPC-driven employment may again rise, the unpredictability of RPC arrangements emphasizes the need to build an adaptable and resilient labor market, including through skills development offered by the APP and seasonal worker schemes. In such a narrow economy, skills development must be especially targeted to market demand, enhancing individual employability.

While the APP allows adults to develop new skills, the government must do more to address the growing problems in youth education. The Nauru Education Strategic Plan 2024–2028—awaiting cabinet approval—envisions an increased role of parents and community engagement for meaningful partnerships to address problems in the education sector, including school attendance. Community and parental support are key to building "education social capital."[10] In May 2024, the governments of Australia and Nauru signed an agreement providing A$1.7 million toward Nauru's education sector to help implement the education sector plan, including supporting Australian-recognized certifications.[11]

By focusing on education, skills development, and community engagement, Nauru can build a more resilient labor market capable of adapting to future challenges and opportunities. Prioritizing human capital will strengthen economic stability, long-term growth, and empowerment for the entire nation.

Notes

[1] Government of Nauru. 2020. *2020 Voluntary National Review on the Implementation of the 2030 Agenda*; International Monetary Fund. 2023. *Republic of Nauru: 2023 Article IV Consultation-Press Release; Staff Report; and Statement by the Executive Director for Republic of Nauru*. IMF Country Report No. 23/376.

[2] Government of Nauru. 2020. *2020 Voluntary National Review on the Implementation of the 2030 Agenda*.

[3] Pacific Community and Government of Nauru. 2023. *Nauru 2021 Population and Housing Census: Analytical Report*.

[4] The 2011 Census showed that 65% of males and 67% of females have English language abilities. The same breakdown by language was not asked in the 2021 Census.

[5] Fiji National University. 2023. *FNU signs MOU with Republic of Nauru's Department of Multicultural Affairs*. Press release. 5 June.

[6] Government of Nauru. 2024. *710 graduate from FNU-certified Alternative Pathways Program. Nauru Bulletin*. Issue 7 – 2024/272.

[7] Government of Nauru. 2024. President Adeang delivers statement on Department of Multicultural Affairs. *Nauru Bulletin*. Issue 10 – 2024/275.

[8] New Zealand Immigration. Recognised Seasonal Employer (RSE) scheme research.

[9] With a significant decline in activity, the RPC shifted to a dormant "enduring capability" mode in July 2023.

[10] Government of Nauru. 2020. *2020 Voluntary National Review on the implementation of the 2030 Agenda*.

[11] Government of Nauru. 2024. *Signing of Australia–Nauru Direct Funding Agreement - Support to Education*.

The North Pacific: Building Resilience in the Renewed Compact Era

Lead authors: Cara Tinio and Kaukab Naqvi

On 9 March 2024, the President of the United States (US) signed into law the third Compact of Free Association (COFA) renewal agreements with all three North Pacific economies (the Marshall Islands, the Federated States of Micronesia [FSM], and Palau).

Based on official releases, the renewed COFAs will channel a total of $7.1 billion in development assistance to these countries over 20 years and continue their access to US federal programs and services. In exchange, the US will retain strategic access to these countries' airspace and waters (United States Congressional Research Service 2024).

The development assistance under the new COFAs—to be provided through direct budget support and increased funding for education, environment and climate change adaptation, health, and infrastructure development—will dramatically increase fiscal resources for the North Pacific economies (Figure 14). The recently concluded COFAs (Compact II) provided a total of $161.5 million in development assistance per year to the three North Pacific economies, equivalent to 20.9% of their average combined GDP during the Compact II period. Under the renewed COFAs (Compact III), total annual assistance—net of trust fund contributions—is estimated at $264.5 million (United States Congressional Research Service 2024). For comparison purposes, this is equivalent to 34.2% of the average combined Compact II GDP.

The execution of the new COFAs promises more generous sector grants and increased contributions to the Compact Trust Funds of the three North Pacific economies, offering vital fiscal opportunities for the governments of these countries as well as potentially large economic benefits. While the additional resources can enhance spending on essential social, infrastructure, and climate adaptation initiatives as well as reduce debts, North Pacific governments must uphold sound fiscal and debt policies and implement reforms to improve PFM capacity. In particular, they should continue to prioritize reforms aimed at bolstering revenue mobilization and enhance expenditure efficiency to elevate the quality of public services.

To fulfil ADB's mandate of promoting economic development and resilience in the Pacific, it is crucial for ADB to collaborate more closely with the North Pacific governments to address capacity constraints. This collaboration should involve tailored approaches that address the specific needs of each country and maximize the impact of interventions by various development partners, including ADB. To support this, it is essential to enhance and improve the policies of these countries, maintaining the momentum of reforms to overcome persistent constraints and promote sustainable economic growth.

All three North Pacific economies face challenges in managing public finances despite ongoing efforts by governments to improve public service quality and fiscal management. To address these issues effectively, both enhancements in public service quality and further fiscal reforms are necessary. For example, post-pandemic, the Palau economy faces elevated debt and historically high inflation. In response, the government ratified the Fiscal Responsibility and Debt Management Act in 2021—which took effect in January 2023—to strengthen PFM (ADB 2024). Similarly, the Marshall Islands remains highly vulnerable to external shocks, including the adverse impacts of climate change, which exacerbates the risk of debt distress. There is a need to improve PFM, establish fiscal buffers, and invest in climate adaptation and disaster risk reduction, although critical reforms are still pending (Graduate School USA 2024). The economy of the FSM also remains highly susceptible to external shocks, such as fluctuations in global commodity prices and extreme climate events. Past experiences highlight the need to strengthen capacity and accelerate PFM reforms to fully leverage growth-enhancing opportunities from COFA resources.

Figure 14: Annual Average Grants to the North Pacific Under the Compacts of Free Association

The new COFAs will increase annual grants to the North Pacific and extend access to US federal programs and services.

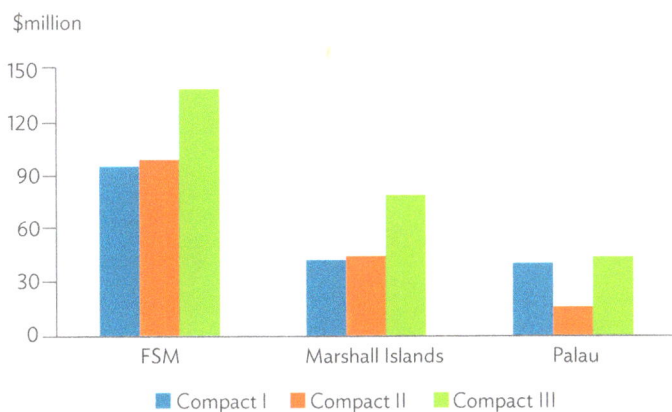

COFA = Compact of Free Association, FSM = Federated States of Micronesia, US = United States.

Notes:
1. The fiscal years (FY) of the Governments of the Marshall Islands, the FSM, and Palau all end on 30 September. Compact I was FY1987–FY2003 for the Marshall Islands and the FSM and FY1995–FY2009 for Palau.
2. Compact II was FY2004–FY2023 for the Marshall Islands and the FSM and is FY2010–FY2024 for Palau.
3. Compact III is scheduled for FY2024–FY2043 for all North Pacific economies. Although Compact II is still in effect in Palau, Palau and the US agreed to start Compact III at the beginning of FY2024 alongside the Marshall Islands and the FSM.

Source: ADB estimates based on the Government of the United States Congressional Research Service. 2024. *In Focus: The Compacts of Free Association*.

Against this background, significant strengthening of PFM is required to ensure that the use of these resources is carefully planned to efficiently and effectively enhance government operations, expand productive public investments, and support more inclusive and sustainable growth and development.

(i)   **Upgrade public investment management.** Strengthening governance and public financial institutions would help ensure that resources provided under the COFA are used efficiently and transparently. Long-term reform agendas are needed to guide medium-term planning and investment, which should, in turn, set development priorities and help identify any complementary interventions and investments that may be needed. Stronger institutions will be better equipped to manage their resources better and implement policies responsive to growing development needs. Further, more robust monitoring and evaluation mechanisms will enhance accountability, identify emerging issues for preventive action, and showcase the impact of COFA-supported public investments.

(ii) **Enhance the quality of public investment.** Strategic investment in other sectors, such as private sector development, and further infrastructure improvements are still needed to complement those funded by the COFA and maximize the development benefits from the additional COFA resources. For instance, improving infrastructure—including planning for the operations, maintenance, and periodic replacement of physical assets—is key to promoting economic growth and increasing resilience and quality of life. These infrastructure enhancements—and measures to foster innovation, support entrepreneurship, and facilitate transactions with the government—would help develop the private sector and diversify the economy.

(iii) **Manage risk.** The increased support for environmental issues and climate change adaptation under the COFA is crucial for the North Pacific economies, which are greatly exposed to rising sea levels and climatic events such as droughts and typhoons. Promoting sustainable agriculture and fishery practices and investing in climate-resilient infrastructure will also be crucial for mitigating the adverse impacts of climate change and disasters. Given the urgency of addressing these vulnerabilities, North Pacific governments should continue seeking support from development partners beyond the COFA with the US to expand available resources and knowledge for crafting and implementing solutions to these complex challenges. Further, allocating more fiscal resources—for instance, through increased contributions to existing trust funds or establishing special-purpose funds—will help strengthen financial resilience to shocks (Noy et al. 2017).

(iv) **Address capacity constraints.** In many small Pacific island countries, including those in the North Pacific, both the working-age and overall populations are relatively small. To address capacity constraints, promoting quality education and skills across the entire workforce is essential. This will strengthen the public sector's ability to efficiently manage and utilize the increased COFA resources and create a skilled private sector workforce capable of maximizing the developmental impact of COFA-supported public investments. Additionally, expanding health care and social services will support worker productivity and resilience to shocks while building human capital.

CONCLUSION AND RECOMMENDATIONS

The increased development assistance anticipated under the renewed COFAs would provide the North Pacific governments with resources, allowing them to enhance their operations, expand public investments, and implement measures that will improve social development outcomes, heighten resilience, and support sustainable and inclusive growth. It is therefore critical to continue strengthening the management of public finances and investments to enable the North Pacific economies to access the expanded resources under the COFA and put themselves in a better position to use these resources to achieve the desired socioeconomic results.

Development partners, including ADB, can play a significant role in supporting this process. They can provide advisory and assessment services to help North Pacific governments gauge the impacts, viability, and feasibility of potential uses for COFA funds, whether in institutional strengthening measures or infrastructure. They can also supplement these COFA resources, including through finding co-financing opportunities, which could support valuable investments that might not be eligible for COFA support or provide emergency assistance, through quick-disbursing facilities, following an extreme climate event or disaster. Finally, development partners can also help supplement public financial and project management capacity on the ground while local capacity is still being developed. ADB stands ready to continue supporting the North Pacific in these areas ensuring that governments can effectively manage and utilize the additional financial resources provided under the new COFAs.

References

ADB. 2024. Palau: Strengthening Fiscal Resilience for Sustainable Development Program, Subprogram 1.

Graduate School USA. 2024. *Fiscal Year 2023 Economic Review.*

I. Noy, C. Tinio, and R. Velasco-Rosenheim. 2017. Financial resilience to disasters: A tool kit. *Pacific Economic Monitor.* December.

United States Congressional Research Service. 2024. *In Focus: The Compacts of Free Association.*

Papua New Guinea Debt Vulnerabilities and Challenges for Debt Sustainability

Lead author: Gholam H. Azarbayejani

Maintaining debt sustainability in Papua New Guinea (PNG) has been a concern for the authorities for over a decade. The "high risk of debt distress"—as assessed in the 2020 through 2023 debt sustainability analyses (DSAs)—cannot all be attributed to the incidence of the COVID-19 pandemic. The upward move of debt indicators during the pandemic resulted from a marked trend of rising public debt during 2013–2024. The government is now more vigilant about potential adverse debt dynamics in the medium to long term. This write-up looks at debt trends of the last decade and recent DSAs conducted jointly by the World Bank and the IMF. Adopting "homegrown" policies and successful implementation of programs and policy actions—as assisted by the country's development partners—points to potential improvement on debt matters and causes optimism.

RECENT DEBT TRENDS

The upward move of PNG's debt-to-GDP ratio since 2020 came on the back of a marked trend of rising public debt during 2013–2024 (Figure 15). The rise from its low of 32.5% of GDP in 2017 to 40.2% in 2019 was the combined result of (i) increased fiscal deficits (Figure 16), which in recent years started in 2018; (ii) the adoption of an internationally accepted definition of public debt to include increases in debt resulting from the revaluation of foreign currencies; and (iii) assumption of interest payment for some guaranteed state-owned enterprise (SOE) project debts.

Figure 15: Papua New Guinea Public Debt Stock, 2013–2024

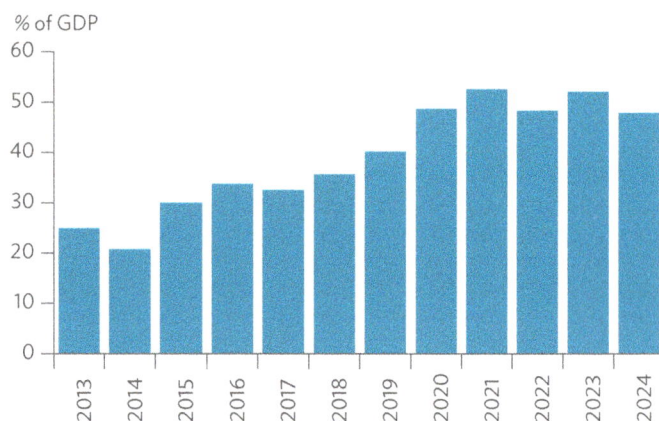

% of GDP

GDP = gross domestic product.

Sources: International Monetary Fund. 2024. *World Economic Outlook April 2024*; and Government of Papua New Guinea, Department of Treasury. 2024. *2023 Final Budget Outcome.*

Figure 16: Papua New Guinea Budget Balance, 2013–2024

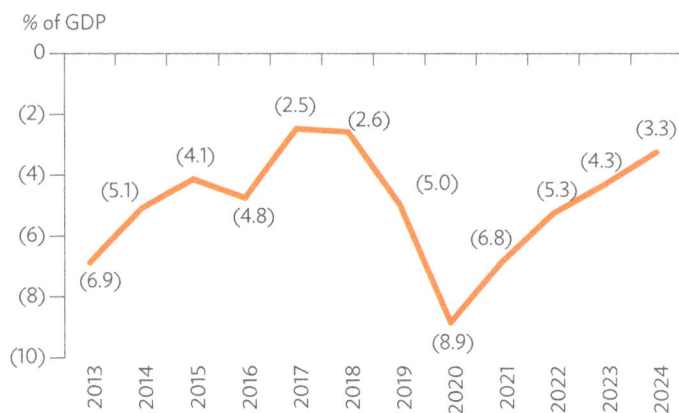

% of GDP

( ) = negative, GDP = gross domestic product.

Sources: International Monetary Fund. 2024. *World Economic Outlook April 2024*; and Government of Papua New Guinea, Department of Treasury. 2024. *2023 Final Budget Outcome.*

Table 3: Papua New Guinea Debt Sustainability Analysis Ratings, 2014–2023

Debt Sustainability Analysis Year[1]	Debt-Carrying Capacity	Risk of External Debt Distress	Overall Risk of Public Debt Distress
2014	Medium Performer[2]	Low	Moderate
2015	Medium Performer	Low	Heightened
2016	Weak Performer	Low	Heightened
2017	Weak Performer	Moderate	High
2018	Medium[3]	Moderate	Moderate
2019 + SMP Request	Medium	Moderate	Moderate
June 2020	Medium	High	High
December 2021 + SMP2 Request	Weak	High	High
May 2022	Weak	High	High
March 2023	Weak	High	High
December 2023	Weak	High	High

SMP = staff-monitored program.

Notes:

1. See the complete debt sustainability analysis (DSA) text at the links in the DSA year above.
2. Country performance ratings are based on the World Bank's Country Policy and Institutional Assessment (CPIA) index used "for the purposes of IMF-World Bank low-income country debt sustainability framework."
3. Starting in 2018, the revised IMF-World Bank DSA framework used a *composite indicator* based on each country's debt profile and its respective CPIA index to determine its debt-carrying capacity. "The medium classification implies that the threshold for the present value of total public debt has increased from 35% to 55% of GDP."

Source: International Monetary Fund and World Bank, Debt Sustainability Analyses, various years.

The events of 2020–2021 heightened PNG's debt woes. Increased financing flows from development partners aimed to contain the devastating effects of COVID-19, the depreciation of the kina, and the sharp deceleration of GDP growth (from 4.5% in 2019 to –3.2% in 2020) all pushed total public debt as a share of GDP to 48.7% in 2020 and 52.6% in 2021. This forced the government to deviate from its medium-term debt strategy and request parliamentary approval of an amendment to the Fiscal Responsibility Act (FRA) that would raise the debt-to-GDP threshold ratio from 45% (set in 2019) to 60% (2020)—the fourth such revision since the FRA's inception in 2006. PNG completed two back-to-back IMF staff monitored programs (SMPs) from February 2020 to June 2021 and, in March 2023, established a 38-month program focusing on— among others—strengthening debt sustainability through sustained fiscal consolidation. As reported in the government's final 2023 budget outcome, the implementation of the government's "budget repair strategy" resulted in public debt declining from its peak in 2021 to 52.0% of GDP in 2023. While below the current FRA-mandated level of 57.5% (set in 2023), this was still well beyond the government's medium-term targets.

CHALLENGES TO DEBT SUSTAINABILITY

In line with the methodology established under the Debt Sustainability Framework for low-income countries, the World Bank and IMF conducted two types of DSAs for PNG: (i) External DSA using public and publicly guaranteed external debts, and (ii) Public DSA using total public liabilities including public sector domestic liabilities.

While all DSAs conducted during 2014–2023 deemed PNG's debt as sustainable under baseline scenarios, stress tests relating to several potential vulnerability factors stemming from combinations of domestic and external sources, in several instances, breached the narrow gap between debt burden indicators and their respective threshold levels. This led to the judgments of "moderate" to "high" risks of debt distress. In the 4 years since 2020, the assessment has stood at a "high" risk of debt distress (Table 3).

In almost all the DSAs listed, the vulnerability factors that contributed to risks of debt distress—in addition to the growth rate of GDP and the size of fiscal deficit—have included exposures to contingent liabilities, commodity price volatilities, upward movements of interest rates, loan currency variations, and incidences of disasters (such as earthquakes, tsunamis, floods, landslides, or fires). These factors, at times, have weakened the fiscal framework, added to fiscal burdens, increased borrowing requirements, and made financing more expensive. To mitigate the risks of these vulnerabilities, the government has often revised its debt management strategies, relying more on concessional external borrowing and extending the maturity profile of its domestic debt securities.

Concerns about PNG's high risk of debt distress have become even more critical as the negative effects of debt vulnerability factors have often affected debt sustainability. Since 2021, PNG's "debt carrying capacity" has been assessed as "weak," requiring a higher standard for sustainability.[1]

VULNERABILITY FACTORS

(i)   **Contingent Liabilities.** The stock of PNG's contingent liabilities has not been closely monitored. A large part of these contingent liabilities is related to explicit guarantees issued by the government to several entities. As of the end of 2022, explicit guarantees were estimated to be equivalent to over 15.6% of total public debt. Of this proportion, 8.6% is owed to domestic sources.

For implicit guarantees, as there is no formal contract, the tendency to neglect their associated fiscal risk can be even higher. For PNG, SOE debt service liabilities do not carry explicit government guarantees. SOE debt consists of two components: (a) debt arising from SOE borrowing from the government as on-lending; and (b) debt arising from SOEs' own borrowing from domestic and external funding sources, which does not require any explicit government guarantees. No specific debt sustainability concerns exist in the on-lending cases, as the original borrowings from which on-lending loans are made are already included in the government debt portfolio. However, when non-payment occurs for SOE direct borrowing—keeping social costs in mind—the government may be forced to absorb the associated budget burdens, as it did in 2020. To the extent that the government feels obligated to engage in SOE financial protection, fiscal risks are elevated, affecting debt sustainability concerns.

To mitigate the risks of contingent liabilities, PNG has taken steps to monitor explicit guarantees and revised its guarantee and on-lending policies. The government has also committed to an ADB-supported SOE reform program that includes restructuring SOE debt and improving SOE efficiency in public finance.

(ii)   **Commodity Prices.** Volatilities in commodity prices have, at times, negatively affected PNG's export earnings as they did when global prices of PNG's major export commodities fell in the second half of 2022. While PNG benefitted significantly from the favorable international commodity prices during 2021–2022—and to some extent in 2023—prices of almost all of PNG's export commodities are projected to decline in 2024, with liquefied natural gas prices expected to fall by 9.0%, and metal prices by 6.0%. The World Bank projects a 4.0% lower global commodity price for 2024, which is likely to fall further by 0.5% in 2025, although a reversal for liquefied natural gas is anticipated in 2025. Further, weaker global demand for PNG's major exports will likely hurt economic growth. Recent DSAs—including the one conducted in 2023—reported that the most extreme shocks (which lead to the highest ratio of present value of debt-to-GDP in the medium to long term) come from export shocks.[2] As such, weak demand for PNG exports and a downward variation in commodity prices have often shown to be external debt vulnerabilities for the country.

(iii)   **Market Risks and Cost of Borrowing.** Market risks that could entail additional fiscal implications often include interest rate risks—closely related to the choice between fixed and floating rate loans—and exchange rate risk from external borrowing.

For PNG, as the total cost of borrowing from domestic sources has been higher than that from external sources, the government strategy since 2016 has relied more on concessional assistance from external development partners. This gradual shift from domestic to external sources has lowered the government interest bill where interest rates on external borrowing—which constitutes about 51.0% of the government debt portfolio—was 2.89% in 2023 against the 5.37% weighted average interest rate for domestic borrowing (Figure 17). This has been a cost/risk trade-off because the shift from domestic to external borrowing increases the risk of foreign currency variations, a vulnerability for the country, and a potential additional budget burden.

(iv)   **Disasters.** PNG has been ranked as one of the most disaster-prone countries in the world due to its unique geo-climate conditions, according to the PNG National Disaster Center. The country has experienced various natural hazards including earthquakes, volcanic eruptions, tsunamis, cyclones, river and coastal flooding, drought, and landslides.[3] PNG's vulnerability increases due to resource constraints and a lack of capacity at various levels. The economic impact of some of these natural hazards could be staggering due to loss of lives and potential production losses that could negatively affect economic growth. To the extent that these disasters have budgetary implications, their effect on fiscal deficit and public debt may become inevitable. Using tools that address the fiscal impacts of natural hazards is advisable to mitigate potential fiscal risks.

Figure 17: Papua New Guinea Shares of External and Domestic Public Debt, 2016–2023

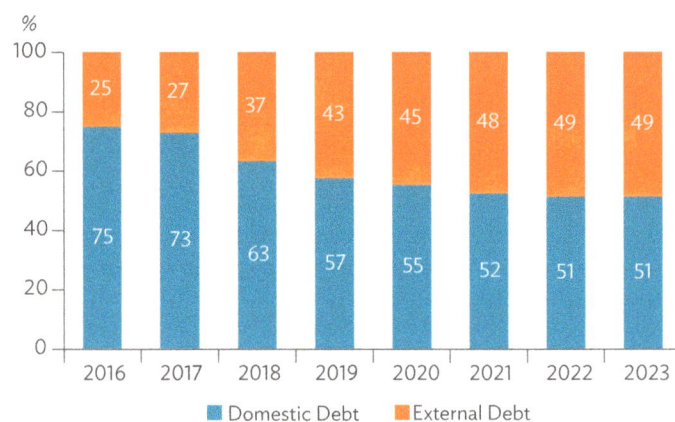

Source: Government of Papua New Guinea, Department of Treasury, National Budget Reports.

CONCLUSION

PNG's public and external debt has remained sustainable, as assessed by various DSAs, during 2014–2023 but there have been several instances—especially during the pandemic years—where the narrow gaps between debt burden indicators and their respective sustainable threshold levels have alerted the authorities about their actual and potential debt vulnerabilities. These vulnerabilities have often stemmed from combinations of domestic and external shocks, including diminished real GDP growth, the size of the fiscal deficit, exposures to contingent liabilities, commodity price volatilities, upward movements of interest rates, variations in loan currency rate, and incidences of disasters, all of which at times have weakened the country's fiscal framework and added to budgetary burdens.

With fiscal consolidation in mind, the government—through its "budget repair" scheme—has expanded the scope of its revenue collection and fortified its expenditure framework. It has also successfully implemented its IMF SMPs and policy actions. While these steps can mitigate some aspects of public debt vulnerabilities, the mitigation process can further benefit from continued strengthening of debt management practices, timely preparation of medium-term debt management strategies that would guide reform and financial directions over the coming years, increased transparency of public financial information, mitigation of risks related to contingent liabilities through enhanced monitoring of public explicit guarantees, and full implementation of newly adopted revised state guarantees and on-lending policies. The use of available tools that address mitigation of risks related to natural hazards—such as disaster risk finance[4]—and those that mitigate risks related to commodity prices and interest rate and currency variations are all strongly advised.[5]

Notes

[1] See the DSA chapter attached to the IMF First Review under Extended Credit Arrangement. 6 December 2023.
[2]. In some DSAs, the most extreme were exchange rate shocks, with export shocks not far behind.
[3] The most recent disaster that afflicted PNG happened on 24 May 2024 when a massive landslide occurred in Mulitaka in Porgera in Enga Province. Hundreds of people were buried alive; the landslide caused significant destruction to buildings, homes, and food gardens and indefinitely blocked the main highway to Porgera Mine.
[4] See the World Bank's Pacific Disaster Risk Financing and Insurance Program.
[5] See, for example, IBRD Financial Products at World Bank Group Treasury.

References

Asian Development Bank. 2022. *The Sustainability of Asia's Debt: Problems, Policies, and Practices.*

Government of Papua New Guinea, Department of Treasury. 2024. *2023 Final Budget Outcome.*

International Monetary Fund. Various Article IV Consultation, DSAs, Staff Reports, 2014–2023 (see links to DSAs in Table 3).

International Monetary Fund. 2023. *Papua New Guinea first reviews under extended arrangement under the Extended Fund Facility and an arrangement under the Extended Credit Facility, Staff Report.*

World Bank. 2023. *Commodity Markets Outlook* October 2023 (accessed June 2024).

World Bank. 2024. *Papua New Guinea Economic Update, May 2024: Invest in Your Children.*

World Bank. n.d. Disaster Risk Financing and Insurance Program.

Reforming Constituency Development Funds in Solomon Islands

Lead authors: Katherine Passmore and Prince Cruz

In this section, SI$ refers to Solomon Islands dollars ($1.00 = SI$ 8.29 as of 1 July 2024).

Solomon Islands first established Constituency Developments Funds (CDFs) over thirty years ago to decentralize development resources and enable Members of Parliament (MPs) to respond directly to constituency needs. However, legislation governing their administration was not introduced until 2013 through a CDF Act.[1] Over their history, CDFs have provided a de facto safety net whereby constituents can seek financial support from MPs as needed, both for immediate and development needs; however, CDFs have long been criticized for lacking transparency and accountability.

Although the Ministry of Rural Development was nominally responsible for administering CDFs, MPs have had almost full control over allocating and disbursing funds to their constituents. Reported uses of CDF funding include covering costs of housing materials, energy and solar supplies, transport, community projects, and education.[2] Some CDF funding has reportedly been used for "individual handouts for their voters" or "direct personal enrichment."[3] Political patronage is common, with some voters reporting that funds are distributed based on political loyalty.[4] With the lack of specific guidelines or laws governing CDF management and expenditure, the funds have been vulnerable to abuse.

In December 2023, Parliament passed a new CDF Act to strengthen governance, transparency, and delivery mechanisms. A key part of the reform shifts much of the decision-making and administration from MPs to civil servants and constituency committees, confining MPs to their roles as legislators and the role of constituency officers to constituency matters.[5] Under the new Act, identifying projects and formulating annual budgets for each constituency is the responsibility of Constituency Development Committees (CDC) and constituency development officers recruited through the Public Service Commission. The Act also stipulates the requirement to adhere to the Public Finance Management Act 2013 and produce publicly available annual reports.

Proponents of the reform describe it as "a home-grown policy… based on actual successes and challenges" encountered in the decades of CDF implementation, incorporating recommendations from Solomon Islanders through a "bottom-up approach."[6] Despite the new administration arrangements and increased involvement of public service-recruited officers, critics of the reform note that "MPs will still be in the driving seat" as they will be involved with the appointment of CDC members and will still need to authorize the signing of cheques and other transactions.[7]

In 2000, the budget allocation for CDFs was about SI$5 million per year before jumping to SI$50 million in 2007 and SI$105 million in 2008 (Figure 18). The budget allocation peaked at SI$374 million in 2017 before falling to an average of SI$250 million per year from 2019 to 2023, and down further to SI$120 million in 2024.[8] These figures represent an average of 20% of the national development budget. Bilateral partners have historically supplemented funding for CDFs.

(iii) Stronger financial, budgetary, planning, and accountability requirements, including that CDFs can only be accessed if a CDC, a development officer, and an accountant are in place;

(iv) Ownership of assets purchased under CDFs will remain with the Ministry of Rural Development;

(v) Requirement for annual constituency conferences and disclosure of financial and implementation reports;

(vi) Introduction of penalties (the 2013 Act had none), including specifying offenses such as misuse of funds and deliberate victimization of non-voters by excluding them from CDF benefits; and

(vii) Introduction of structured guidance on fund allocation with specific percentages designated for productive and resources sectors (40%), essential services (20%), cross-sector initiatives and inclusivity (20%), and social and cultural obligations (20%).

Figure 18: Solomon Islands Constituency Development Fund

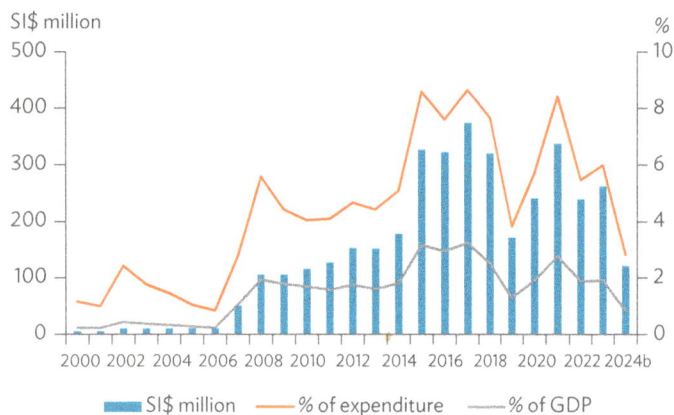

b = budget, GDP = gross domestic product, SI$ = Solomon Islands dollars.
Source: ADB estimates using Solomon Islands budget documents and International Monetary Fund Article IV staff reports.

Figure 19: Solomon Islands Public Perception of Constituency Development Funds, 2019

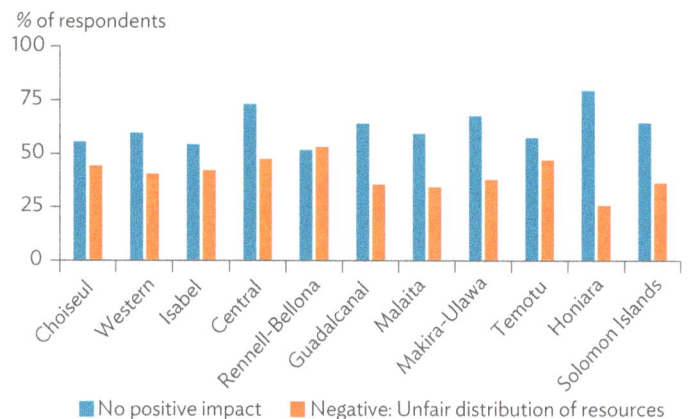

Note: Respondents were asked "What is the main area of development assistance that the CDF has contributed *positively* whether directly or indirectly to your household?" A separate question asked how CDF contributed *negatively*.
Source: Government of Solomon Islands. 2023. *2019 Population and Housing Census: National Report (Volume 1)*.

Despite the relatively large allocation for CDFs, the 2019 Census generally reported negative community perceptions of the funds. Of 130,000 respondents, 64% said that the CDF had no positive impact on them (Figure 19). Dissatisfaction with the fund was relatively higher in Honiara, Central Province, and Makira-Ulawa. The most commonly cited negative impact of CDFs was the "unfair distribution of resources" (36%).[9] The top three suggestions for future management of CDFs were good governance, prosecution of corrupt officials, and improved coordination.

Other significant changes under the CDF Act 2023 included:[10]

(i) A clear statement of the purpose and principles of the Act;

(ii) The introduction of CDCs to manage CDFs, comprising at least five members, two of whom must be female, ensuring more inclusive decision-making;

The new CDF Act provides opportunities to minimize corruption and political patronage, while enhancing resource allocation transparency, governance, and inclusivity. These reforms address many of the criticisms and challenges faced under the previous legislation, but true reform will be seen in implementation. While MPs will retain some level of control, the reforms give the public more tools to hold their elected representatives to account. Successful implementation of the reforms and a practical reduction in political influence will be critical to the effective and equitable use of CDFs, ultimately leading to improved development outcomes and enhanced public trust. In the context of limited fiscal space and rising public debt, efforts to improve the utilization of scarce financial resources are most welcome.

Notes

1. F. Fono. 2007. A perspective on constituency development in Solomon Islands. *Pacific Economic Bulletin*. 22 (2). pp. 127–130. Australian National University.
2. Government of Solomon Islands. 2023. *2019 Population and Housing Census: National Report (Volume 1)*.
3. G. Kekea and A. Ride. 2023. *How Constituency Development Funds Undermine Solomon Islands' Democracy*. United States Institute of Peace. 25 October.
4. C. Wiltshire, J. Batley, J. Ridolfi, and A. Rogers. 2020. Constituency Development Funds and electoral politics in Solomon Islands: part one. *Devpolicyblog*. Australian National University Development Policy Centre. 7 September.
5. Government of Solomon Islands. 2023. *Constituency Development Funds Bill 2023 (No. 17 of 2023)*.
6. Government of Solomon Islands, Ministry of Rural Development. 2023. *Cabinet approves Constituency Development Policy, CDF legislation next*. 19 March.
7. Transparency Solomon Islands. 2023. *Transparency Solomon Islands On The Constituency Development Funds Bill 2023*. 18 December.
8. Government of Solomon Islands. 2023. *2024 Development Budget*.
9. Government of Solomon Islands. 2023. *2019 Population and Housing Census: National Report (Volume 1)*.
10. Government of Solomon Islands. 2024. *New CDF law enforced*; Government of Solomon Islands. 2023. *Constituency Development Funds Bill 2023 (No. 17 of 2023)*.

Navigating Turbulence: Air Vanuatu and the Future of Air Travel in Vanuatu

Lead authors: Katherine Passmore and Prince Cruz

In this article, Vt refers to Vanuatu vatu ($1.00 = Vt120.38 as of 1 July 2024).

After Air Vanuatu suspended its operations in May 2024, other regional airlines stepped in to ensure continued connectivity for Vanuatu: an act of Pacific resilience. This write-up provides a brief insight into Air Vanuatu's recent performance, emphasizes its significance in supporting tourism and economic activity, and highlights the support provided by neighbors to restore connectivity.

PATH TO VOLUNTARY ADMINISTRATION

Government-owned Air Vanuatu has long faced financial difficulties. From 2006 to 2019, losses reached Vt4.7 billion, requiring large financial injections and write-offs from the national government (Figure 20). In 2019, the government released an ambitious tourism development plan that included expanding the Air Vanuatu fleet, but the COVID-19 pandemic hampered these ambitions. Air Vanuatu registered a Vt2.2 billion net loss in 2020, and in March 2021, the government took direct control of Air Vanuatu for restructuring.[1] Political instability added to the problem as there was a lack of clear direction from the government and frequent changes in the Air Vanuatu board.

Figure 20: Air Vanuatu Net Operating Profit or Loss

GDP = gross domestic product, Vt = Vanuatu vatu.
Source: G. Wong. 2022. National Airline or National Burden?? *Vanuatu Business Review*. September.

On 9 May 2024, the government put the airline under voluntary administration to be overseen by Ernst and Young (EY).[2] The initial liquidator's report noted that Air Vanuatu was "unable to meet the costs of parts critical to fleet operations, resulting in grounded aircraft and reduced revenue."[3] At the government's direction, the key priorities were to determine assets and liabilities, ensure employees were taken care of, and manage risks and suppliers.

ECONOMIC IMPACTS

Air Vanuatu has played a significant role in Vanuatu's economic and social development. Operating in 28 airports on 20 islands, the airline provided critical air links from the capital, Port Vila, to major tourism destinations, Santo and Tanna, and rural areas. In 2019, Air Vanuatu reported directly contributing over 7% of Vanuatu's GDP.[4] In 2023, it provided about 75% of international flights and employed more than 400 Ni-Vanuatu.

Following the decision to place Air Vanuatu in administration, ADB's forecast of GDP growth has been lowered to 1.9% (from 3.1% in *ADO April 2024*) for 2024 and to 2.4% (from 3.6%) for 2025, with substantial downside risks (Figure 21). The immediate impacts are expected to be seen in sectors directly affected by tourism, such as accommodation and restaurants, wholesale and retail trade, and transportation. While regular international links to Port Vila were restored relatively quickly, as of 8 August 2024, domestic connectivity remains limited. The impact on tourism in outer islands and local employment will likely be extensive.

Figure 21: Vanuatu Supply-Side Contributions to GDP Growth

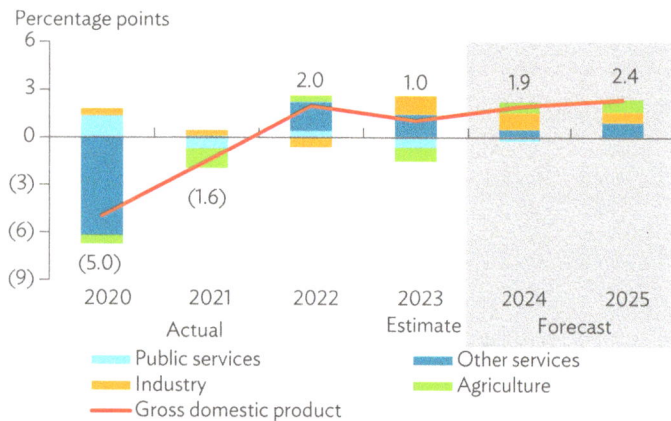

Source: ADB estimates.

A survey of 378 businesses on the impact of the Air Vanuatu collapse found that:

- 92% of respondents had been affected;
- 70% of respondents reported a 30% or more decline in turnover;
- Accommodation and restaurants, tour operators, transport, retail, and real estate businesses were most affected; and
- 91% of accommodation providers reported lower occupancy rates than the previous year, while 88% of tour operators reported lower bookings.[5]

DEBT SUSTAINABILITY

A significant concern about Air Vanuatu's collapse is the potential impact on the Government of Vanuatu's debt position. After Cyclone Pam hit the country in 2015, Vanuatu's external debt increased rapidly to finance reconstruction and infrastructure upgrades. Since then, debt has been extremely close to (or in breach of) the external debt ceiling of 40.0% of GDP (Figure 22). Although Vanuatu was able to prepay some debt—leading to a decline in debt in 2022—external debt is expected to rise again to finance reconstruction following cyclones in 2023. Reconstruction needs are estimated at 36.7% of GDP, although this figure includes reconstruction for damages from previous cyclones (including the 2020 tropical cyclones Pam and Harold).[6]

In its 2023 Article IV consultation, the International Monetary Fund (IMF) identified significant contingent liability risk associated with Air Vanuatu: "Large cost overruns and an overambitious investment plan involving the order of six Airbus aircraft resulted in losses and brought the viability of the airline into question....the airline remains in severe financial distress." The debt sustainability analysis accompanying the 2023 Article IV report reconfirmed IMF's assessment that Vanuatu was at moderate risk of external and overall debt distress but with "limited space to absorb shocks." The IMF did not include Air Vanuatu in the analysis due to lack of data.[7]

The liquidation process is revealing the extent of Air Vanuatu's debt. An early assessment by the liquidator in May 2024 estimated total known liabilities of $73.5 million (about 7.4% of GDP), with

$26.6 million owed to "unsecured creditors" and $21.8 million to the Government of Vanuatu. The debt to the government is likely to be written off as a loss equivalent to 2.2% of GDP. Aside from the unknown employee entitlements, the liquidators anticipate that "It is likely the value of liabilities will increase materially."[8] If these liabilities are recognized on the government's balance sheet, there will be added pressure on the public debt burden in the short term in an already constrained fiscal space. Assuming that the government does not recapitalize the airline, ceasing ongoing financial support to a loss-making entity will provide some reprieve in the longer term. The fiscal balance has been tight since the pandemic, with an average deficit of 3.4% of GDP in 2020-2022. A major source of revenue—the Honorary Citizenship Program (HCP)—has been declining for several years and is not expected to recover due to uncertainty regarding its main attraction: visa-free entry to the European Union and the United Kingdom. In June 2024, the European Union finalized the revocation of visa-free entry for Vanuatu passport holders. HCP revenues plummeted to Vt8.1 billion (6.9% of GDP) in 2023, far below the peak of Vt14.4 billion (13.7%) in 2020. HCP revenues in the first half of 2024 were way below the target.

Figure 22: Vanuatu External Debt

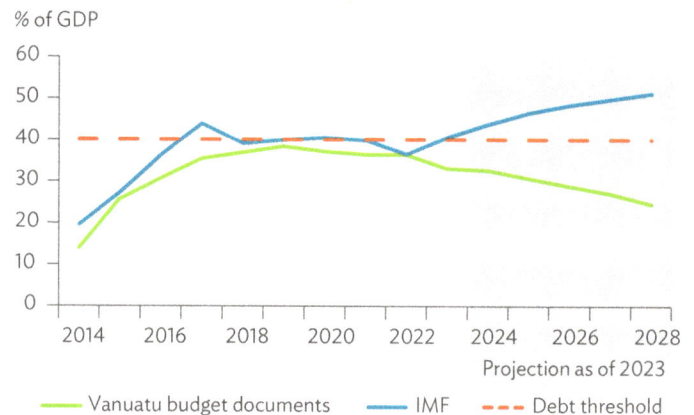

GDP = gross domestic product, IMF = International Monetary Fund
Sources: IMF Article IV report (various years); and Government of Vanuatu. Ministry of Finance and Economic Management budget documents.

RECONNECTING VANUATU

With the collapse of Air Vanuatu, other regional airlines have increased their capacity or flight frequency to quickly restore international connectivity, which has been made possible by proactive responses from local and international authorities. In May, Fiji Airways upgraded the aircraft on its Suva to Port Vila service from an ATR 72 to a Boeing 737 (adding 110 seats per flight) to accommodate additional demand. Virgin Australia also increased its flights from Brisbane to Port Vila from three to five times a week in May, and in July, it increased further to seven times a week, with a possibility of adding flights during peak season.[9] In June, the Government of Vanuatu signed an agreement with Nauru Airlines to restore flights from Brisbane to Santo and Port Vila.[10] Solomon Airlines has also increased the frequency of international flights to Vanuatu.

Meanwhile, Qantas and Jetstar have received approval to provide air services from Australia to Vanuatu for the next 5 years, with routes and frequency expected to expand over the coming months.[11]

The administration has also spurred domestic private sector aviation activity. For instance, a privately owned company providing chartered flights from Port Vila applied in June 2024 for a license to offer regularly scheduled flights.[12] It also acquired a new aircraft to increase its capacity, which will go some way to helping restore domestic connectivity.

While the initial hit to tourism by the administration of Air Vanuatu is expected to be significant, the expanded flight coverage to Vanuatu may boost the tourism sector in the medium term. Although international connectivity has been restored—reportedly with a net increase in seats—domestic connectivity is still being addressed.

CONCLUSION

Air Vanuatu has played an important role in connecting Vanuatu—both internationally and domestically—and supporting the development of the tourism industry, which is crucial to the economy. However, given its historical financial performance and reliance on government support, its demise is not entirely unexpected. The direct and indirect economic impacts are expected to be significant in the short term, particularly as domestic connectivity remains limited. However, the swift action of other airlines to restore international connectivity will help to buffer the impacts on tourism and may catalyze more private sector aviation activity, strengthening consumer confidence over the medium term.

Rather than subsidizing a loss-generating airline, the government could consider this an opportunity to encourage private sector competition and investment in aviation. International examples provide valuable lessons for encouraging private sector activity in aviation after the collapse of a national airline. The experience of Air Vanuatu also provides a broader lesson on the management of state-owned enterprises, emphasizing the importance of reforms that champion a private sector orientation and the need to avoid pouring scarce resources into unsustainable enterprises. The draft Government Business Enterprises Bill in Vanuatu seeks to address these issues but has been awaiting approval by Parliament since 2018. The recent developments with Air Vanuatu signal the need to prioritize the approval and implementation of this legislation.

While the connectivity issues are being resolved, the government's fiscal and debt sustainability is of great concern. While the extent of Air Vanuatu's liabilities is still being determined, it is unclear how these liabilities will be financed and what the trade-offs will be. The 2024 national budget was coined "the capital budget" because it focuses on capital investments. Capital expenditure is essential for growth, including ongoing tourism development; however, overall government expenditure must be carefully examined in the context of Air Vanuatu's liabilities. As the already limited fiscal space reduces—compounded by declining HCP revenues—there is an urgent need to diversify and expand sources of revenue.

While the liquidation process is expected to be completed by August 2024, there remains significant uncertainty over the future of Air Vanuatu. A positive outcome in an otherwise extremely challenging circumstance is the regional effort to keep Vanuatu connected during a crisis, an example of Pacific resilience.

Notes

1 iCOUNT Accountants Consultants Advisors. 2021. *Audited Financial Statements: Air Vanuatu (operations) Limited 1 January 2020 to 31 December 2020.*
2 EY. 2024. *Air Vanuatu (Operations) Limited (In Liquidation) - Statutory Liquidators Report Update.* 17 May.
3 EY. 2024. *Minutes of Meeting of Creditors: Air Vanuatu (Operations) Limited (In Liquidation).*
4 R. Butler. 2020. Air Vanuatu handles record passengers and achieves record revenue in 2019. *All About Vanuatu.* 27 February.
5 Vanuatu Chamber of Commerce and Industry. 2024. *How the Air Vanuatu crisis has affected our Industry sectors.*
6 ADB. 2024. *Asian Development Outlook April 2024.*
7 IMF. 2023. Vanuatu: 2023 Article IV Consultation. *IMF Country Report* No. 23/115.
8 EY. 2024. *Liquidators' Statutory Report to Creditors pursuant to Section 44 (1) of the Companies (Insolvency and Receivership) Act No. of 2013 ("the Act") Air Vanuatu (Operations) Limited (In Liquidation).* 14 May.
9 Virgin Australia. 2024. Virgin Australia lifts Vanuatu capacity. Trade release. 24 June.
10 ABC. 2024. Vanuatu Govt hopes to restore international flights with Air Nauru. 11 June.
11 Vanuatu Tourism Authority. 2024. Getting to Vanuatu.
12 *Vanuatu Daily Post.* 2024. Air Taxi acquires new Islander aircraft, seeks approval for regular flights. June 18.

POLICY BRIEFS

Bolstering Climate Resilience in the Pacific Islands

ABSTRACT

Climate change significantly impacts small island developing states (SIDS), which are highly vulnerable due to their low elevations. Effective climate adaptation and adequate financing are essential for these communities to manage climate risks. The social-ecological resilience (SER) framework—which integrates human and natural systems—offers a foundation for enhancing resilience in SIDS. Policy and macro-fiscal considerations are fundamental for increasing adaptive capacity and reducing climate risks. The Asian Development Bank (ADB) promotes the Pacific Approach and differentiated strategies for SIDS and fragile and conflict-affected situations (FCAS) contexts in the Pacific. Enhancing social cohesion and opportunities for vulnerable populations is critical. Innovative strategies are necessary, such as public-private partnerships (PPPs), pro-poor PPPs (5Ps) initiatives, and community-based adaptation mechanisms (CoBAMs). A comprehensive approach combining policy measures, financial strategies, and community engagement is essential for building resilience in SIDS.

1. Introduction

Climate change disproportionately impacts communities, severely affecting SIDS and Pacific island countries (PICs), which are used interchangeably in this write-up. The urgency to understand and implement successful adaptation strategies has never been higher. Addressing climate adaptation and ensuring adequate financing is essential for these communities to cope with climate change risks.

SIDS—as a distinct group of developing countries—face significant vulnerability to climate change and sea-level rise, especially the atoll countries (Kiribati, Republic of the Marshall Islands, and Tuvalu) due to their low elevations in average two meters above sea level, and fragile ecosystems, particularly susceptible to the impacts of climate change. The effects of sea-level rise in SIDS include the loss of land and coastal erosion, intensified coastal flooding due to tides, storms, and waves, and rising salinity in coastal aquifers. This situation has led to a decrease in habitats, the migration of coastal species, a decline in biodiversity, and a reduction in ecosystem services such as providing cultural goods and services associated with natural capital such as coral reefs, mangroves, or forests. Among humans and infrastructure, the impacts include home loss, population displacement, loss of lives and livelihoods, disturbance in economic sectors, heightened water insecurity, and interruptions to crucial infrastructure such as transport and communication. According to the Intergovernmental Panel on Climate Change (IPCC, 2019), high sea-level rise scenarios on some Pacific islands could exceed the technical limits of hard protection, with economic and social barriers emerging before these technical limits are reached (Figure 1).

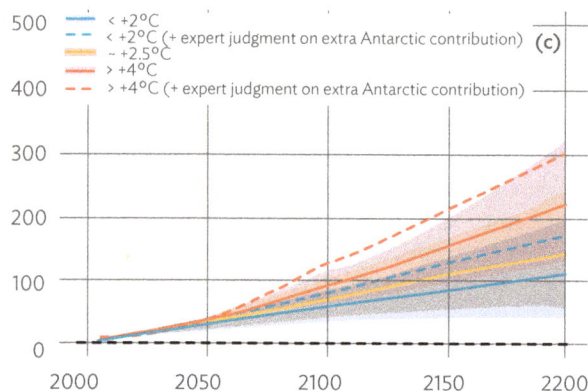

Figure 1: Projections of Local Sea-Level Rise (cm) Until 2200 for Kiribati

°C = degrees Celsius (or centigrade), cm = centimeter
Source: R. Martyr-Koller,et al. 2021. Loss and damage implications of sea-level rise on Small Island Developing States. *Current Opinion in Environmental Sustainability*. 50. pp. 245–259.

An example from one SIDS country, Kiribati, as shown in Figure 1, illustrates the severe impact of sea-level rise. If temperatures follow a 2.5 degrees Celsius trajectory, sea levels could potentially increase by nearly 1 meter by 2100 compared to the current scenario.

An important issue in building a resilience framework under climate change is differences in the perception of the risks among decision-makers, planners, and communities. Literature articulates that implementing a multifaceted adaptation strategy calls for both preventive and remedial actions, especially in the context of nature-based solutions that are likely to contribute to medium- and long-term climate change adaptation, also referred to as nature's contributions to adaptation (Turner et al., 2022).

2. Building Climate Resilience

Resilience frameworks can guide the planning and implementation of bolstering resilience in Pacific islands, especially considering the unique context of SIDS and FCAS. ADB has found that the small, isolated, and dispersed nature of these areas presents key challenges: narrow and vulnerable economies, long distances from key markets, capacity and governance barriers, higher infrastructure costs, and inequality in accessing services among rural–urban and vulnerable populations (ADB 2021a).

Building on the social-ecological systems (SES) framework (Holland, 1995, and Holling, 2001) in literature and the IPCC 2014 definition of resilience as "the ability of a system and its component parts to anticipate, absorb, accommodate, or recover from the effects of a hazardous event in a timely and efficient manner, including through ensuring the preservation, restoration, or improvement of its basic structures and functions," Turner et al. (2022) augmented the concept to the social-ecological resilience (SER) framework. The authors defined SER as the "capacity of SES to withstand desired outcomes in the face of disturbance and change, by both buffering shocks and adapting or transforming in response to change."

In the context of framing SER for multilateral development bank (MDB) investments and approaches, a World Bank report (2020) outlined several key principles for adaptation and resilience: establishing frameworks for implementation, monitoring and evaluation, focusing on national budgets for adaptation expenditures and related economic damages, and considering the timing and severity of hazard risks and/or climate change shocks. These principles also emphasize the need to identify beneficiaries, as outlined in the recently adopted *MDBs' Common Approach to Measuring Climate Results* (World Bank, 2024), which specifies resilience beneficiaries as a set of key stakeholders, including people, firms, and ecosystems, disaggregated by attributes such as gender, poverty level, and geographic coverage.

Linking resilience beneficiaries to broader development outcomes and impacts requires the SER framework to vary by scale, context, and depth. A "one-size-fits-all" approach is not recommended, particularly for the Pacific, where a differentiated approach calls for context-sensitive interventions, flexible processes, enhanced operational approaches, strengthened capacity and partnerships, and a focus on sustainability and resilience (ADB, 2021b). The fragmented investment approach will not suffice for these highly vulnerable areas.

Assessing climate change risks, vulnerability, and resilience of economic systems implies that nature-dependent sectors like ecotourism or fisheries are likely to be affected by the state of habitats and climate change exposure. For ecotourism—particularly the hospitality sector dependent on coral reef ecosystems—effective management actions to reduce vulnerability by protecting and restoring ecosystems will enhance resilience. Similarly, subsistence and commercial fisheries depend on economic instruments such as fishing quotas, water quality, and fisheries stock. A bio-economic modeling of coral reef ecosystems with tourism or fishing revenue is needed to identify externalities influencing the economic value of protecting and restoring SES systems.

For the Pacific, balancing the economic development of community livelihoods with natural resource endowments through adaptation and nature's contributions to adaptation is vital. By examining the extent of financing in increasing adaptive capacity through the SES and resilience lens, leveraging economic instruments and incentives can significantly impact SES. However, these economic instruments and incentives must consider nature's complexities that vary over scales and change over time (Levin et al., 2013).

Preventive actions involve implementing adaptation measures in anticipation of climate change effects, while remedial actions focus on responding to impacts already occurring. Considering the perception of risk around bounded rationality versus rational thinking, there is a need to anticipate the adverse effects of hazards such as floods and droughts, as in the case of bounded rationality. Preventive investments in climate-change adaptation—funded by taxes or reduced spending in other areas—can increase the resilience of capital stock, maintain manageable public debt dynamics, and ensure adequate fiscal space to cope with natural disasters while responsibly accessing international capital markets.

2.1 Challenges in "Bouncing Back" and Recovering from Disasters and Climate Change Impacts

Key challenges in Pacific island countries (PICs) include recovering and rebuilding when hit by the effects of compounding climate change and disaster risks. These challenges include:

(i) Micro: Low adaptive capacity for communities highly dependent on the environment and/or nature or the ecosystem.

A study by Nunn and McNamara (2019) found that climate change impacts resulting from coastal flooding disrupt communities dependent on fisheries and agriculture in Fiji. These events have often necessitated relocation, considered a local-level adaptation instead of a complete failure to adapt (Betzold, 2015). Similarly, in Vanuatu, communities reliant on agriculture and fishing—including informal workers and many women artisans selling handicrafts at the Port Vila market—face climate-related challenges such as flooding, coastal erosion, and drought. These communities are addressing their predicament through adaptation initiatives such as building seawalls to prevent land loss and installing rainwater tanks for water harvesting to enhance water security.

(ii) Macro: Lack of public and private financing.

The isolation, scattered geography, and small populations of PICs result in high public service delivery costs and disproportionately large public sectors compared to their economies. For low-lying atoll nations like Kiribati and the Marshall Islands, annual climate adaptation investments could surpass 20% of their gross domestic product (GDP), while for most other PICs, these investments are estimated at 5% and 10% of GDP (World Bank, 2016; cited in ADB, 2018). Limited public sector budgets and restricted access to capital markets make it difficult to secure the necessary funds, leading to over-reliance on global aid.

3. Solutions and Recommendations

Policy and macro-fiscal considerations can significantly increase adaptive capacity and reduce exposure to climate change risks, mainly through differentiated approaches. ADB emphasizes the need for the *Pacific Approach* and a differentiated approach within the FCAS context, where six of the 14 Pacific island countries—Kiribati, the Marshall Islands, the Federated States of Micronesia, Nauru, Solomon Islands, and Tuvalu—are classified *FCAS*.

Enhancing social cohesion and opportunities in communities and strengthening social resilience to violence, climate extremes, and natural disasters—especially for the most vulnerable populations (older people, women, persons with disabilities, and children)—are critical goals. The *Pacific Approach, 2021–2025*, aims to foster resilience in the region by (i) enhancing preparedness and response to shocks, (ii) ensuring the provision of sustainable services, and (iii) promoting inclusive economic growth (ADB, 2021b). In this context, programmatic approaches—such as ADB's policy-based loans—are aimed at implementing reforms and, in some cases, investments to tackle transformational adaptation interventions.

In the Fifth Assessment Report, the IPCC (2014) characterized fundamental system changes in response to climate change and its socioeconomic effects. The subsequent Sixth Assessment Report by the IPCC (2022) further developed transformational adaptation, which underscores a systems approach that involves adjustments in both human and natural systems due to climate change and its associated impacts. Hence, transformational adaptation requires innovative and integrated strategies that go beyond conventional boundaries, enhancing resilience to the unpredictability of climate change. There is an urgent necessity for heightened investment and strategic planning in climate adaptation and building resilience in investments, communities, and nature to realize transformational adaptation. This approach is crucial to bridge the expanding gap between the pressing needs and the available finance, especially in developing countries (UNEP, 2023).

Some suggestions for key policy-level measures for beneficiaries include actions that can result in transformational adaptation and resilience.

(i) Private Investment

Transformational adaptation investments may involve multiple actors, sectors, or assets, making the scale and complexities larger. Given that public resources are limited, there is a strong case for encouraging private sector investment, such as PPPs, where the public sector finds avenues to create incentives to engage the private sector in financing climate-resilient infrastructure. De-risking facilities or risk-reducing measures—along with other MDB harmonized approaches to reduce climate-induced risks in SIDs—can enable an environment to unlock opportunities to access concessional financing and insurance services and products scalable at low transaction costs. The 5Ps initiatives or business model is a great avenue for climate insurance products for the most vulnerable and informal sectors in PICs, especially for the agriculture sector where key stakeholders engage in creating community and individual-based products against climate-induced disasters (Jain et al., 2022).

Financing instruments that leverage technology and capacity building with CoBAMs should also be considered. Building capacity, training, and advisory services around climate change, environment, social, and governance—along with digitalized platforms with big data and diagnostic tools—can inform communities, businesses, and countries in preparing for climate and disaster events. Rational

decision-making for protection mechanisms is typically based on a cost-benefit analysis of stand-alone investments or individual assets; thus, there is a need for bounded rationality thinking in anticipating the risks (Camerer, 1999).

(ii) Community and Individuals

Facilitating CoBAMs in creating and pursuing adaptation outcomes valued by livelihoods, learning from traditional governance systems, coping strategies, and indigenous knowledge is important for transformational adaptation (McNamara et al., 2020). Addressing cross-sector impacts on the workforce and the need for reskilling is also relevant. As a form of transformational adaptation, one approach is pursuing risk-based planning to establish a coastal setback zone, by creating a buffer to reduce the climate change risks to communities.

Coastal settlement relocation or migration represents a more extreme form of adaptation, where communities including their infrastructure and livelihoods, are relocated to less vulnerable locations to climate-proof against future risks. This process may involve livelihood reconfiguration and economic and cultural changes, making migration a valuable instrument for SIDS to cope with climate- related damages, especially where natural capital degradation is irreversible. Financial transfers through remittances can help, but migration is disruptive and comes with welfare costs. Policymakers should consider the implications for both local inhabitants and migrants when designing policies to address climate-related damages (Cassin et al., 2022).

In a Nunn and McNamara (2019) study in Vanua Levu Island, Fiji, 19 families were relocated from Denimanu Village to Korovou on Yadua Island, Bua, in 2016. They gained modern facilities such as solar panels and water tanks and installed flush toilets and showers. Similarly, the villagers from Vunidogoloa were moved to Kenani in 2014, where the new location facilitated commercial opportunities but faced erosion issues due to construction. Both relocations in Fiji aimed to improve living conditions and accessibility.

(iii) Fiscal Policies: Debt Sustainability and Public Budget

Early investment in adaptation is pivotal for SIDS, which are most vulnerable to the impacts of climate change. By combining public adaptation spending with public debt reduction or the accumulation of savings in a reserve fund, these countries can increase the resilience of their capital stock and improve financial sustainability. This approach can ease future borrowing constraints, ensuring these nations remain financially stable and better equipped to handle climate-related challenges (Catalano et al., 2020). Importantly, donors have to play a part in reducing the public debt-to-GDP ratio, creating reserve funds, and securing donor grants for maintaining stable GDP growth while managing the impacts on national debt levels.

Balancing public and concessional financing is also critical for small island countries to manage the financial burden of adaptation spending. Leveraging capital markets and mobilizing domestic resources are critical steps in this process. However, this is limited to a few sizeable or larger economies in SIDS such as Papua New Guinea and Fiji. Access to concessional or blended financing facilities—either as direct investments or as mechanisms to mitigate risks (de-risk) through concessional capital, guarantees or risk insurance, and technical assistance funds—is necessary. These financial instruments can support adaptation projects, ensuring that these countries can effectively respond to and recover from climate-related impacts.

In bolstering climate resilience, it is challenging to attribute climate-related and non-climatic drivers and impacts—such as adverse effects of infrastructure development and human-induced habitat degradation—directly to climate risks. However, there is a need to examine further the modeling aspects of nature, economic and social impacts attributed to climate change with other non-economic parameters that are implicit or intangible, such as biodiversity or ecosystem services losses that are not traded in markets, including cultural heritage, indigenous knowledge, social values, and their tipping points.

Lead author: Sabah Abdulla, senior economist (climate change), Economic Research and Impact Evaluation Department, ADB, with inputs from Alessio Giardino, senior climate change specialist (coastal adaptation), Climate Change and Sustainable Development Department, ADB.

References

Asian Development Bank (ADB). 2021a. *Pacific Approach, 2021–2025.*

ADB. 2021b. *Building a differentiated approach for fragile and conflict-afflicted situations and small island developing states: Briefing note for consultations.*

C. Betzold. 2015. Adapting to climate change in small island developing states. *Climatic Change.* 133(3). pp. 481–489.

C. Camerer. 1999. Behavioral economics: reunifying psychology and economics. *Proc Natl Acad Sci U S A.* 96(19). pp. 10575–10577.

L. Cassin, P. Melindi-Ghidi, and F. Prieur. 2022. Confronting climate change: Adaptation vs. migration in Small Island Developing States. *Resource and Energy Economics.* 69. p. 101301.

M. Catalano, L. Forni, and E. Pezzolla. 2020. Climate-change adaptation: The role of fiscal policy. *Resource and Energy Economics.* 59. p. 101111.

L. H. Gunderson and C. S. Holling. 2002. *Panarchy: understanding transformations in human and natural systems.* Island Press.

J. H. Holland. 1995. Hidden order. *Business Week-Domestic Edition.* 21.

C. S. Holling. 2001. Understanding the Complexity of Economic, Ecological, and Social Systems. *Ecosystems.* 4(5). pp. 390–405.

Intergovernmental Panel on Climate Change (IPCC). 2014. Fifth Assessment Report.

IPCC. 2019. Sea Level Rise and Implications for Low-Lying Islands, Coasts and Communities.

IPCC. 2022. Sixth Assessment Report.

D. K. Jain et al. 2022. Climate risk insurance in Pacific Small Island Developing States: possibilities, challenges and vulnerabilities—a comprehensive review. *Mitigation and Adaptation Strategies for Global Change.* 27(3). p. 26.

S. Levin et al. 2013. Social-ecological systems as complex adaptive systems: modeling and policy implications. *Environment and Development Economics.* 18(2). pp. 111–132.

R. Martyr-Koller, et al. 2021. Loss and damage implications of sea-level rise on Small Island Developing States. *Current Opinion in Environmental Sustainability.* 50. pp. 245–259.

K. E. McNamara et al. 2020. An assessment of community-based adaptation initiatives in the Pacific Islands. *Nature Climate Change.* 10(7). pp. 628–639.

P. D. Nunn and K. E. McNamara. 2019. Failing adaptation in island contexts: the growing need for transformational change. *Dealing with climate change on small islands: towards effective and sustainable adaptation.* Gottingen University Press. pp. 19–44.

B. Turner et al. 2022. The Role of Nature-Based Solutions in Supporting Social-Ecological Resilience for Climate Change Adaptation. *Annual Review of Environment and Resources,* 47. pp. 123–148.

United Nations Environment Programme (UNEP). 2023. *Adaptation Gap Report 2023.*

World Bank. 2016. *Climate and Disaster Resilience.* Pacific Possible Background Report No. 6. Quoted in ADB. 2018. *Pacific Economic Monitor,* December.

World Bank. 2020. *The Adaptation Principles: 6 Ways to Build Resilience to Climate Change.*

World Bank. 2024. *Joint MDB Methodological Principles for Assessment of Paris Agreement Alignment.*

Resilient Infrastructure—The Pacific Way

INTRODUCTION

There are significant challenges for Pacific developing member countries (DMCs) in financing, building, and maintaining vital infrastructure, particularly given ongoing development challenges and the proneness of Pacific DMCs to the impacts of climate change and natural disasters. This paper briefly outlines some challenges and opportunities facing infrastructure development in Pacific DMCs and how Pacific DMCs address those challenges: resilient infrastructure, the Pacific way.

Economic and social development challenges are not unique to Pacific DMCs. Still, the challenges are often exacerbated in Pacific DMCs due to issues including relatively low resource endowments, relatively low levels of human capital, poor access to trading markets, a lack of economies of scale and scope for reducing economic diversification of risks, relatively high costs of business inputs, inequality of opportunity and services between urban and rural populations, and increasing risks of climate change. This often leads to shortfalls in the provision of essential infrastructure services. For example:

(i) Sustainable Development Goal (SDG)[1] 06—relating to safe and managed drinking water access—indicates that the percentage of the population with access across Pacific DMCs ranges from about 50% to almost 100%. However, there is often significant variation in outcomes within individual Pacific DMCs (e.g., the percentage in Papua New Guinea [PNG] in urban areas is almost twice that of rural areas, a testament to service delivery difficulties across such challenging and diffusely populated terrain).

(ii) Sustainable Development Goal 07—relating to access to electricity—indicates that the percentage of the population with access to electricity ranges from about 20% to 100%. Again, significant differences often exist between urban and rural areas. However, disadvantages in remote locations are often less insurmountable than water services due to alternative energy and off-grid energy technologies.[2]

Robust infrastructure and reliable infrastructure services are vital to underpinning economic and social development in areas including international trade, domestic commerce, housing, food security, health, education, workforce productivity, and general improvements in quality of life. In short, empirical evidence shows a positive correlation between per capita indicators of infrastructure provision and gross domestic product (GDP) and, subsequently, broader economic and social outcomes. Furthermore, investment in infrastructure and the operations of infrastructure and associated services are major contributors to economic activity and welfare across the Pacific.

Resilient infrastructure is a more holistic approach to infrastructure delivery that ensures the resilience of the infrastructure itself, the resilience of communities and businesses reliant on the infrastructure, and the resilience of the decision-making, ownership, and operation of the infrastructure in the long term.

There has been an increasing focus on climate-resilient infrastructure that serves two purposes:

(i) Infrastructure for resilience: This is infrastructure planned, designed, and delivered to ensure communities and societies are resilient

(ii) Infrastructure that is resilient: This infrastructure is resilient to climatic shocks and stresses.

THE SCALE AND SCOPE OF THE INFRASTRUCTURE CHALLENGE IN THE PACIFIC

Based on performance against metrics such as SDGs, significant scope exists for greater investment in resilient infrastructure across Pacific DMCs. Estimates from 2015 indicate that the infrastructure investment needs in the Pacific were $60.0 billion, or $4.0 billion per annum when adjusted to 2024 prices. When factoring in the additional cost of climate change mitigation and adaptation, those estimates increase to $65.0 billion ($4.4 billion annually), which does not include the costs attributable to the risks of sea level rise. Considering these figures, these requirements exceed 8.0% of subregional GDP.

Infrastructure requirements vary significantly across the subregion. Several initiatives identify, scope, and prioritize the infrastructure investment needs across the Pacific. One key initiative is the National Infrastructure Investment Plans (NIIPs), multisector infrastructure plans developed by individual Pacific DMCs with the assistance of the Pacific Region Infrastructure Facility (PRIF). NIIPs identify and consolidate a pipeline of infrastructure projects across all sectors and thematic issues plans into one plan. Projects are identified, scoped, and prioritized based on their alignment with Pacific DMC strategic development needs and objectives to provide a list of projects for investment and development. More detailed designs and business cases are subsequently developed to support budget request submissions and potential funding from development partners. Most Pacific DMCs completed NIIPs in 4 years to 2023, including the Cook Islands, Fiji, Kiribati, Nauru, Niue, Palau, Samoa, Solomon Islands, Tonga, Tuvalu, and Vanuatu. Other NIIPs will be completed by early 2025, and existing NIIPs will be periodically reviewed and updated.

Many Pacific DMCs also have specific sector plans (e.g., transport, energy, or information and communication technology) or issue-based plans (e.g., National Adaptation Plans for climate change adaptation) and investment strategies that complement and/or include specific projects embedded within the NIIPs process.

These NIIPs, sector plans, and thematic plans collectively provide a consolidated picture of the pressing and emerging infrastructure needs across the Pacific. While a fully consolidated pipeline of all infrastructure projects is not available as of July 2024, even the 190 economic infrastructure projects included within the PRIF member pipelines that are likely to be deployed in the short term (in the next 1–2 years) would require an investment of approximately $5 billion (noting this excludes all projects from PNG and social infrastructure projects such as education and health infrastructure). Figure 3 shows the distribution of these infrastructure projects by sector, indicating that almost half of the projects by number are attributable to transport (25%) and water and sanitation (23%), but noting many projects are multisector.[3] These projects are all under more detailed consideration and only represent a fraction of the identified infrastructure development needs.

Figure 3: Distribution of Economic Infrastructure Projects by Sector in Pacific Developing Member Countries

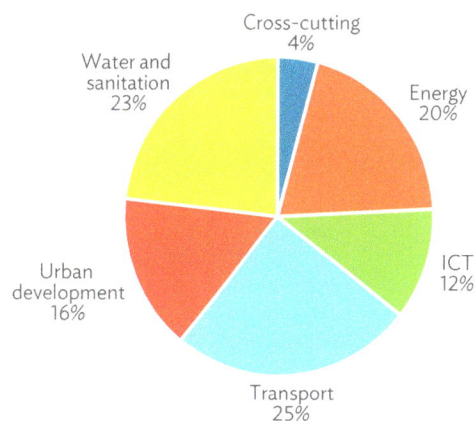

- Cross-cutting 4%
- Energy 20%
- ICT 12%
- Transport 25%
- Urban development 16%
- Water and sanitation 23%

ICT = information and communication technology.

Note: Pacific developing member countries included in pipeline data are the Cook Islands, Fiji, Kiribati, the Republic of the Marshall Islands, the Federated States of Micronesia, Nauru, Niue, Palau, Samoa, Solomon Islands, Tonga, Tuvalu, and Vanuatu.

Source: Pacific Regional Infrastructure Facility analysis.

RESILIENT INFRASTRUCTURE THE PACIFIC WAY— THE PACIFIC QUALITY INFRASTRUCTURE PRINCIPLES

There has been a greater recognition that addressing infrastructure requirements requires a more nuanced approach to recognizing the scale, scope, and diversity of circumstances and challenges in the Pacific. Recognizing the disproportional climate risks in the region and the need to mainstream social and environmental safeguards into infrastructure, the Pacific Islands Forum endorsed the Pacific Quality Infrastructure Principles (PQIPs) in November 2023, which specifically embed resilience:

Adopting the PQIPs should improve the resilience of infrastructure provision and services throughout the project cycle.

In a practical sense, these principles build on a legacy of work and initiatives across the Pacific to enhance the deployment of investment development and operation of infrastructure for the people and economies of the Pacific. Furthermore, these principles provide a more holistic lens through which resilient infrastructure is defined and delivered in Pacific DMCs, where resilience goes beyond the direct physical attributes of the infrastructure and considers a broader suite of resilience attributes articulated through the principles.

Overview of Pacific Quality Infrastructure Principles

Promote sustainable, local, and inclusive economic development, including greater access to jobs, business, and training opportunities for Pacific Islands people.

This principle should ensure that a greater proportion of the economic benefits of investment are captured within Pacific developing member countries (DMCs), further underpinning economic development. Practical applications of this principle include:

- Context-specific contract design, packaging of works, and prioritization of local participation where value for money can still be achieved. For example, the Asian Development Bank (ADB) utilizes a differentiated approach to partnering with Pacific DMCs to reflect local context and needs.
- Targeted investment in capacity building and training to enable greater levels of participation by Pacific people and businesses.

Other initiatives are also being considered that could enhance local contractor access to insurance, greater visibility of the pipeline of future infrastructure investments to mitigate information asymmetry between funding agencies and contractors, and matching international and local contractors to undertake projects jointly.

Integrate value-for-money principles across asset life cycles to ensure financial considerations are balanced against non-financial objectives such as quality and generating sustained social and economic benefits for local communities.

This principle ensures a longer-term and broader view of value is used when assessing and financing infrastructure projects. This includes strategies such as:
- More emphasis on estimating and incorporating lifecycle costs within project identification and scoping by Pacific DMC governments within their national infrastructure investment plans.
- More focus on maintaining and renewing infrastructure assets to maximize economic life and reduce lifecycle costs.
- Procurement practices that both enhance local content and develop local capacity, ultimately leading to greater competition and downward pressure on project costs.

Ensure projects are resilient to future impacts of climate change and natural disasters and are fully aligned with the Pacific's international commitments and agreed pathways toward 2050 net-zero emissions under the Paris Agreement.

Implementing this principle is being delivered through several significant initiatives, including:
- The emphasis on alternative energy sources across Pacific DMCs, particularly where they have inherent technical and cost advantages, such as in remote locations.
- Greater emphasis on identifying, scoping, and incorporating climate risks into infrastructure design and implementation and/ or specific infrastructure projects to mitigate the risk to other economic and social assets (e.g., seawalls and ecosystem-based adaptation projects as part of infrastructure portfolios)
- Greater preparedness for natural disasters and, to the extent possible, betterment of infrastructure when rebuilt post-natural disaster.

Soft infrastructure further underpins these initiatives, such as research, data and tools, benchmarking, building codes, capacity building, direct assistance in project design and delivery, greater coordination of resilience activities across Pacific DMCs and development partners, and specific climate financing such as the Global Climate Fund.

Support sound public financial management, debt transparency and project-level and country-level debt sustainability. Ensure good governance, including transparent procurement, protections against corruption, and opportunities for local participation in governance/oversight.

Significant emphasis has been placed on greater discipline for asset management and maintenance, governance, financial management, tariff implementation (when feasible), appropriate and sustainable debt financing, and infrastructure delivery and management transparency across Pacific DMCs. This has included concerted efforts by Pacific DMC governments and utilities with support from development partners.

Issues of governance and appropriate financing (such as grants, loans, and public-private partnerships) are fundamental to infrastructure provision in Pacific DMCs. These will continue to drive efficiencies and a broader suite of funding opportunities for private sector participation that reflects project risks and opportunities.

Incorporate in all projects' applicable standards on social and environmental safeguards.

Social and environmental safeguards are increasingly being mainstreamed into infrastructure development and associated services through social and environmental impact assessments at the core of project due diligence, and direct actions to mitigate impacts as part of project delivery. These initiatives are usually requirements for most development partner-supported infrastructure and increasingly for infrastructure projects delivered by Pacific DMC governments.

Promote non-discriminatory access to infrastructure services, and ensure inclusion of women, people with disabilities, Indigenous Peoples, and underrepresented groups in the design and delivery of infrastructure projects.

Increasing emphasis is now placed on enhancing inclusivity in the design, delivery, and operations of infrastructure and associated services. Gender equality, disability, and social inclusion are emerging as key considerations in infrastructure development. Research, guidelines, capacity building, and coordination across stakeholder groups and infrastructure providers are occurring, but much more effort will be required to mainstream inclusivity.

Promote market-driven and private sector-led investment, supported where appropriate by judicious use of public funds, as the most efficient driver of sustainable quality infrastructure development.

Geography, scale, cost, capacity, and income and/or affordability create significant challenges for fully commercial and market-driven infrastructure services in Pacific DMCs. Despite this, opportunities do exist and are pursued wherever possible. This is particularly so for Pacific DMCs such as Fiji and PNG, where larger customer bases exist, and for services where market-led delivery of services is more commercial (e.g., communications, energy, large-scale transport).

This principle is progressing through multiple initiatives, including institutional and regulatory reforms within Pacific DMCs and creating more appropriate investment environments through contracts with private sector entities for infrastructure service delivery. Its success will depend on the degree to which the other Pacific Quality Infrastructure Principles are achieved, notably greater local content, value for money, and responsible borrowing and governance.

CASE STUDIES

The following two case studies outline some recent examples of how resilience has been mainstreamed into infrastructure projects in the water and electricity sectors in Kiribati and Tonga.

Case Study 1: Kiribati—South Tarawa Water Supply

The Problem

South Tarawa, the capital of Kiribati, is home to over 60,000 people (half of Kiribati's population). The string of islets that make up South Tarawa is very low-lying, and the islets are very densely populated. Water resources are limited and dominated by water lenses (groundwater) at Bonriki and Buota. These sources form part of a public and private portfolio of water supply assets, including household-scale rainwater harvesting and small-scale wells. However, these resources face several challenges:

- They are insufficient in volume to meet the population's needs, with water access to potable water by households being heavily restricted.
- Water quality is severely compromised, resulting in major incidences of waterborne disease, particularly among vulnerable population cohorts such as infants.
- Climate change is further exacerbating the adequacy and reliability of water sources. This includes increased climate variability (drought impacting rainwater harvesting yield and reliability and aquifer recharge) and rising sea levels, which increase the risks of seawater intrusion into groundwater lenses. Furthermore, increases in peak temperatures will increase water demand and place further pressure on climate-dependent water resources.

Inaction would continue to increase the economic and social risks due to deteriorating supply and increasing demand.

Solution and Status

A water supply solution that is climate resilient (independent), reliable, and safe is required. Climate-dependent water supplies cannot meet these needs. Analysis and consultation found that the only feasible solution to meet the service needs at scale was a desalination solution (the South Tarawa Water Supply Project). However, given the significant energy requirements for desalination, the water supply project has been integrated with an alternative energy solution (the South Tarawa Renewable Energy Project). The solution has been funded by the Government of Kiribati, ADB, the World Bank, and the Green Climate Fund, with an estimated cost of $58 million (2018 prices).

Much of the project design, site preparation, and early work have been completed, and the project is moving to the major stages of construction.

Outcomes

The principal outcome of the project is a larger-scale, climate-resilient, safe, and reliable water source. In delivering the project, several other resilience elements are also being implemented that align with the Pacific Quality Infrastructure Principles. These include:

- Reduced waterborne diseases that contribute to poor health outcomes that also have flow-on social and economic impacts. These risks can be acute in vulnerable cohorts of the community, including infants, older people, and those with disabilities. This also places significant pressure on the health budget. Research undertaken in 2012 estimated the economic cost of water-borne disease in South Tarawa to be $4.0 million–$7.8 million per annum (2024 values)—equivalent to 2.0%–3.8% of GDP.
- Reduced net carbon emissions. The project is estimated to avoid about 89,400 tons of carbon dioxide emissions over its life due to the use of solar energy for the desalination plant and households' ability to reduce fossil fuel use to boil water to ensure it is suitable for potable use. Based on estimates of the social cost of carbon emissions, the economic value of reduced emissions is about $5.1 million.
- Social issues have been assessed, and social safeguards implemented throughout the development process. These included a specific resettlement plan and compensation for the small number of households displaced in the development footprint.
- Specific initiatives to enhance local content in the development and operation of the desalination plant include training and capacity building as part of the works package and contracts for subsequent operation and maintenance.
- Responsible governance is achieved through local oversight and capacity building via the National Water and Sanitation Steering Committee, while capacity building across Pacific DMCs is achieved via the Pacific Water and Wastewater Association's annual conference.
- Responsible financial management and affordability are embedded in the project through the proposed tariff structures and support for meeting operating expenditures over its useful life.

Source: Global Climate Fund. 2018. Funding Proposal. FP091: South Tarawa Water Supply Project. Kiribati | Asian Development Bank (ADB) | Decision B.21/34.

Early works for the South Tarawa Water Supply Project and water ranks used for the current approach (photos by Karim Eldib).

Case Study 2: Tonga—Cyclone Gita Recovery Project (energy sector)

The Problem

Tonga is a country of 172 islands (36 inhabited) with a total population of about 107,000. Almost 70% live on the main island of Tongatapu, home to the country's capital of Nuku'alofa. Based on a country's exposure, susceptibility, coping, and adaptive capacities, the World Risk Report 2021 ranked Tonga as the third country (next to Solomon Islands and Vanuatu) most vulnerable to natural hazards, such as tropical cyclones and storm surges. Such disasters have inflicted significant losses on Tonga's economy while straining its public expenditure. Rising sea levels, ocean temperatures, and other climate-induced effects have played a major role in increasing Tonga's exposure to natural hazards.

On 12 February 2018, Tropical Cyclone Gita made landfall in Tonga. It was the most intense storm ever to hit the island nation. It disrupted communities and damage to the energy sector on the islands of Tongatapu and 'Eua was estimated at about $7.3 million. The total recovery and reconstruction cost with the "building back better" approach was estimated at $149 million, of which $46 million was allocated for the energy sector, including the reconstruction of power grid infrastructure assets on Tongatapu to a higher standard of disaster resilience.

Six weeks after the cyclone, businesses and schools remained closed as Tonga Power Limited (TPL) worked on reconnecting 17,800 customers in Tongatapu through temporary emergency repairs awaiting permanent reconstruction and disaster-proofing. Restoring reliable electricity supply in priority areas throughout reconstruction and upgrading was vital for essential services and minimizing secondary economic impacts.

Solution and Status

In June 2018, the Asian Development Bank (ADB) and the Government of New Zealand approved grants for a project to reconstruct and improve disaster resilience of the Nuku'alofa electricity network in partnership with the Government of Tonga and TPL. The project closed in December 2020, costing $9.4 million.

The project delivered impacts toward more reliable and safe energy services, reduced energy consumption, increased resilience to disasters, and more dependable and safer buildings and structures to improve services and maintenance. The project utilized several innovations and good practices to help de-risk the electricity infrastructure's exposure to climate and disaster risks. For example:

- Tonga's new solution of using aerial bundled cables for high-voltage and low-voltage networks was deemed more resilient than running three separate bare conductors.
- Trenched underground connections were used for vital social infrastructure such as hospitals and other customers where feasible.

These initiatives were designed to mitigate the consequences of future cyclones on infrastructure and enable the return of electricity services more quickly after a major natural disaster.

Outcomes

The de-risking initiatives implemented after Tropical Cyclone Gita paid material dividends during Cyclone Harold in April 2020.

The upgraded sections of the network sustained minimal damage from the impact of Cyclone Harold in comparison with the damage suffered by sections that remained to be upgraded. For example:

- Services were maintained and/or reinstated more quickly for vital customers.
- The bundled cables proved stronger and more resilient in bearing the weight of falling trees and flying debris, as witnessed during the cyclone event.

During the delivery of the initiative, other outcomes consistent with the Pacific Quality Infrastructure Principles were also achieved, including:

- A 50% reduction in infrastructure faults and outages during routine operations in Nuku'alofa, reducing lifecycle costs of service delivery and economic and social losses to the community and businesses attributable to outages.
- Significant local content and opportunities for local contractor involvement through the use of smaller contract packages that were within the capacity of local contractors.
- TPL's Environmental and Social Safeguards Unit considered and delivered social safeguards. In addition, women comprised about one-third of the workforce on the project, which is relatively high for engineering-dominant projects.

While this initiative was primarily a betterment project to de-risk energy infrastructure, it has delivered a broader scope of resilience across ongoing operations, capacity development, and governance of energy infrastructure.

Source: ADB. 2022. Completion Report. Tonga: Cyclone Gita Recovery Project.

Installation of electric conduits on building walls and maintenance activities of energy infrastructure in Tonga (photos by ADB).

MOVING FORWARD—RESILIENT INFRASTRUCTURE THE PACIFIC WAY

The needs and challenges for effective and efficient infrastructure development, operation, and service provision in the Pacific are as diverse as the geography and people of the region. Resilience is at the center of better infrastructure outcomes in the long term. The PQIPs provide a more holistic framework through which resilience is considered in the Pacific, going beyond climate resilience to include broader economic, social, governance, and private sector participation outcomes. While the PQIPs may make the delivery of infrastructure projects more complex in the short term, the long-term net benefits will be positive.

Lead author: Jim Binney and Katherine Baker, Pacific Region Infrastructure Facility.

Notes

[1] Sustainable Development Goals are an initiative adopted by United Nations members that provides a framework and measurable development metrics (including for infrastructure service provision) that measure development progress.

[2] Pacific Data Hub (accessed 20 June 2024).

[3] The distribution of budget by sector is not possible based on existing data due to a lack of budgets for several projects.

References

Australian Infrastructure Financing Facility for the Pacific. 2024. *Learning and Discussion paper: Local Content. Unpublished.*

Asian Development Bank (ADB). 2014. *Economic Costs of Inadequate Water and Sanitation, South Tarawa, Kiribati.* https://www.adb.org/publications/economic-costs-inadequate-water-and-sanitation-south-tarawa-kiribati

ADB. 2017. *Meeting Asia's infrastructure needs.* https://www.adb.org/publications/asia-infrastructure-needs

ADB. 2017. Guidelines for the economic analysis of projects. https://www.adb.org/documents/guidelines-economic-analysis-projects

ADB. 2017. *Resettlement Plan. Kiribati: South Tarawa Water Supply Project.* https://www.adb.org/projects/documents/kir-49453-001-rp

ADB. 2019. *Environmental Assessment Document. Kiribati: South Tarawa Water Supply Project.* https://www.adb.org/projects/documents/kir-49453-001-eia

ADB. 2020. *Public–Private Partnership Monitor: Papua New Guinea.* https://www.adb.org/publications/public-private-partnership-monitor-png

ADB. 2021. *Pacific Approach 2021-25.* https://www.adb.org/sites/default/files/institutional-document/712796/pacific-approach-2021-2025.pdf

ADB. 2022. *Completion Report. Tonga: Cyclone Gita Recovery Project.* https://www.adb.org/projects/documents/ton-52129-001-pcr

Coalition for Disaster Resilient Infrastructure. n.d. *Compendium of Good Practices on DRI – Case Study: Cyclone Gita Recovery Project.*

Global Climate Fund. 2018. *Funding Proposal. FP091: South Tarawa Water Supply Project. Kiribati | Asian Development Bank (ADB) | Decision B.21/34.* https://www.greenclimate.fund/document/south-tarawa-water-supply-project

Global Facility for Disaster Reduction and Recovery. *Tonga: Post-Disaster Rapid Assessment.*

Pacific Island Forum. 2023. *Forum Communiqué.* Prepared for the Fifty-Second Pacific Islands Forum Rarotonga, Cook Islands. 6–10 November 2023. https://forumsec.org/sites/default/files/2024-03/52nd%20Pacific%20Islands%20Forum%20Communique%2020231109.pdf

Pacific Island Forum. 2023. *Pacific Quality Infrastructure Principles. Summary Principles.* https://forumsec.org/sites/default/files/2024-02/Pacific%20Quality%20Infrastructure%20Principles.pdf

Pacific Region Infrastructure Facility (PRIF). 2021. *Pacific Infrastructure Performance Indicators 2021.* https://www.theprif.org/document/regional/infrastructure-performance/pacific-infrastructure-performance-indicators-2021

PRIF. 2021. *A Shared Approach for Management of Environmental and Social Risks and Impacts for Pacific Island Countries.* https://www.theprif.org/document/regional/gender-and-social-safeguards/shared-approach-management-environmental-and-social

PRIF. 2021. *Pacific Infrastructure Maintenance Benchmarking Report. 2021 Baseline Assessment.* https://theprif.org/document/regional/infrastructure-maintenance/benchmarking-infrastructure-maintenance-pacific-island

PRIF. 2022. *Guideline to Preparing National Infrastructure Investment Plans.* https://www.theprif.org/national-infrastructure-investment-plans

PRIF. 2022. *Enhancing Procurement Practice and Local Content Pacific Infrastructure.* https://www.theprif.org/document/regional-guidance-prif/local-content/enhancing-procurement-practice-and-local-content

PRIF. 2022. Inclusive Infrastructure in the Pacific: Study on Gender Equality and Social Inclusion. https://www.theprif.org/document/regional/gender-and-social-safeguards/inclusive-infrastructure-pacific-study-gender

PRIF. 2022. *Guidance for Managing Sea Level Rise Infrastructure Risk in Pacific Island Countries.* https://www.theprif.org/news/thu-03172022-1042/guidance-for-managing-sea-level-rise-infrastructure-risk-pacific-island

PRIF. 2024. *Value for Money Procurement for Pacific Infrastructure.* Forthcoming.

PRIF. 2024. *Insurance Risk Management and Insurance in the Pacific.* https://theprif.org/document/regional/infrastructure-insurance/insurance-risk-management-and-insurance-pacific

K. Rennert et al. 2021. *The Social Cost of Carbon: Advances in Long-Term Probabilistic Projections of Population, GDP, Emissions, and Discount Rates.*

Tetra Tech. 2024. *Pacific Infrastructure Market: Barriers, enablers and interventions.* Forthcoming.

Public Financial Management and Economic Resilience

INTRODUCTION

Public Financial Management (PFM) encompasses the principles governing the laws, institutions, systems, and procedures governments utilize to optimize the efficient allocation of economic resources to enhance public service quality. Strategic investment in fundamental infrastructure is imperative for stimulating economic growth and resilience, maximizing the efficacy of public investment, and achieving enhanced service delivery. Nevertheless, inadequacies in PFM and public investment management systems can hamper countries from fully realizing their long-term growth potential.

Given the important role of the public sector in most Pacific economies, effective financial management within the sector is crucial for delivering public services and fostering economic resilience. Weak PFM systems limit the ability of Pacific governments to ensure the effectiveness and efficiency of expenditures in implementing macroeconomic policies. PFM reform in Pacific developing member countries (DMCs) is essential but particularly difficult due to their unique developmental challenges, which include small domestic markets, high transportation costs, and vulnerability to disruptions such as disasters and trade volatility.

Factors affecting economic resilience—the ability of economies to recover from adverse shocks—vary between advanced and emerging economies. For example, research indicates that in advanced economies, a flexible exchange rate regime can strengthen resilience. In emerging economies with limited flexibility in exchange rates and higher foreign currency-denominated debts, it is recommended to focus on maintaining sufficient foreign exchange reserves to enhance economic resilience (Eichengreen et al., 2024).

The public sector must uphold effective fiscal positions to foster sustainable and resilient growth. Budget execution in Pacific DMCs is frequently disrupted by the reallocation of expenditure during the year as both foreseeable and unforeseeable priorities come to the forefront, such as unforeseen spending pressures stemming from disasters or other abrupt developments. Viewed in this context, ensuring sufficient contingency allocations in the budget and fortifying PFM assumes heightened significance. Reinforcing PFM and public sector management is pivotal in enhancing the efficiency and effectiveness of public expenditure and promoting economic resilience.

Although the link between strengthening PFM and economic resilience is complex, empirical evidence (International Monetary Fund [IMF], 2015) demonstrates a positive correlation between the quality of PFM systems, aggregate fiscal discipline, and budget credibility. While analyzing the impact of public investment on the size and quality of public infrastructure, this research finds that approximately 30% of potential gains from public investment

are lost due to inefficiencies in public investment processes. This supports the viewpoint that a well-functioning PFM system—with the introduction of fiscal discipline—can improve the effectiveness of public investments and potentially enhance the quality of public services. However, the economic and social impact of public investment critically depends on its efficiency.

The maintenance of robust macroeconomic and fiscal fundamentals holds the utmost significance. Unproductive government spending yields adverse implications, whereas productive government spending establishes positive feedback between the economy's productive capacity and tax revenues. Proficient fiscal management holds the potential to bolster economic resilience and sustain growth (Daniel and Gao, 2015). In an economy that experiences variations from its typical trajectory of stable growth, deficit financing may have the potential to stimulate growth. However, it is crucial to recognize that fiscal stimulus—leading to increased public spending and poor financial management—can harm growth potential by increasing debt levels and possibly leading to a debt crisis (Adam, 2004). While government spending can help during recessions, its effectiveness in promoting a strong recovery is limited in economies with high public debt levels. Pacific DMCs facing a high risk of debt distress will have to pay more attention to improving the quality of public sector management to support productive investments.

Empirical evidence broadly supports the view that recoveries tend to be prolonged and slower in a weak pre-crisis financial system, particularly when a financial crisis accompanies the recession (Reinhart and Rogoff, 2009). This finding is supported by Kannan et al. (2009), who assert that timely interventions can significantly impact the duration and severity of a recession and the strength of the subsequent recovery. The economic resilience of Asian economies during the 2008–2009 global financial crisis was attributed to favorable initial conditions, controlled credit expansion, and enhanced bank asset quality. Robust macroeconomic fundamentals and prompt implementation of financial regulations and supervision also played pivotal roles in this resilience. Asian economies expeditiously revised financial regulations and bolstered supervisory mechanisms for financial institutions, mitigating risk-taking activities by households and firms before the global financial crisis and ultimately reinforcing economic resilience (Phakawa et al., 2014).

Evidence suggests that implementing financial reforms in urban areas may yield positive spatial spillover effects, enhancing economy-wide resilience (Jian et al., 2024). A comprehensive study encompassing 65 countries using data from 1985 to 2015 indicates that the effective enforcement of fiscal, expenditure, and debt regulations—coupled with improved institutional performance—can play a significant role in attaining macroeconomic stability (Afonso et al., 2022).

Reinforcing PFM and improving institutional quality can be crucial drivers in fostering economic growth and resilience. Robust institutions serve as catalysts, amplifying the positive influence of financial development on economic growth. PFM fosters economic development by facilitating efficient capital mobilization, financial intermediation, and capital formation. Enhancing PFM systems can also reduce costs by providing essential information pertinent to potential investment considerations and facilitating improved resource allocation (Fengju and Assmamawu, 2024).

LONG-TERM GROWTH POTENTIAL AND ECONOMIC RESILIENCE

An empirical analysis of the Pacific subregion's long-term actual and potential growth rates can provide valuable insights into achieving sustainable and resilient growth.[1] Recognizing the importance of enhancing a country's potential growth has critical implications for promoting sustainable and resilient development. Improving capacity to produce a wide range of goods and services is crucial to raising living standards, reducing inequality, ensuring debt sustainability, and achieving resilient and sustainable economic growth.

To comprehend the Pacific subregion's capacity to withstand diverse external demand shocks and achieve economic resilience, an empirical analysis comparing the actual GDP growth rate with the potential growth rate—characterized as the maximum GDP growth rate sustainable without creating inflationary pressures—and the balance-of-payments-constrained growth rate (BOP-constrained), i.e., the growth rate consistent with a balanced current account can provide valuable policy insights (Figure 4).

The basic concept of "BOP-constrained growth" states that no country can grow faster in the long term than the rate compatible with the current account balance unless it can finance ever-growing deficits. If financial inflows grow faster than GDP, the ratio of external debt-to-GDP will eventually increase. However, there is a limit to the debt-to-GDP ratio before international financial markets become nervous about the risk of debt distress. Consequently, there is a growth rate that a country cannot exceed in the long term without causing balance of payments problems. This is the "BOP equilibrium growth rate" (Thirlwall, 1979). This suggests that maintaining a current account balance within a manageable range is critical to keeping the external debt-to-GDP ratio sustainable and avoiding debt distress. However, this limits actual and potential growth rates. Sustainable economic growth cannot exceed the rate consistent with the current account balance, shown in Figure 4 as the BOP-constrained growth rate.

Analysis shows that actual economic growth in the 1990s in Pacific DMCs averaged 4.2%. This growth rate fell to 2.2% in the 2000s and rose to 4.4% during 2010-2019 before turning negative in 2020 (5.7%) and 2021 (1.5%). The analysis also shows that actual GDP growth—estimated at 3.3% during 1990-2022—was very close to the BOP-constrained growth rate estimated at 3.2%, with fluctuations observed over the years.

Average economic growth during 1990-2022 remained lower than the potential growth rate estimated at 3.6%. Moreover, the potential and actual growth rates declined before the coronavirus disease (COVID-19) shock, indicating limited productive capacity.

Figure 4: Pacific Developing Member Countries' Actual, Potential, Balance-of-Payments-Constrained Growth Rates (1990-2022)

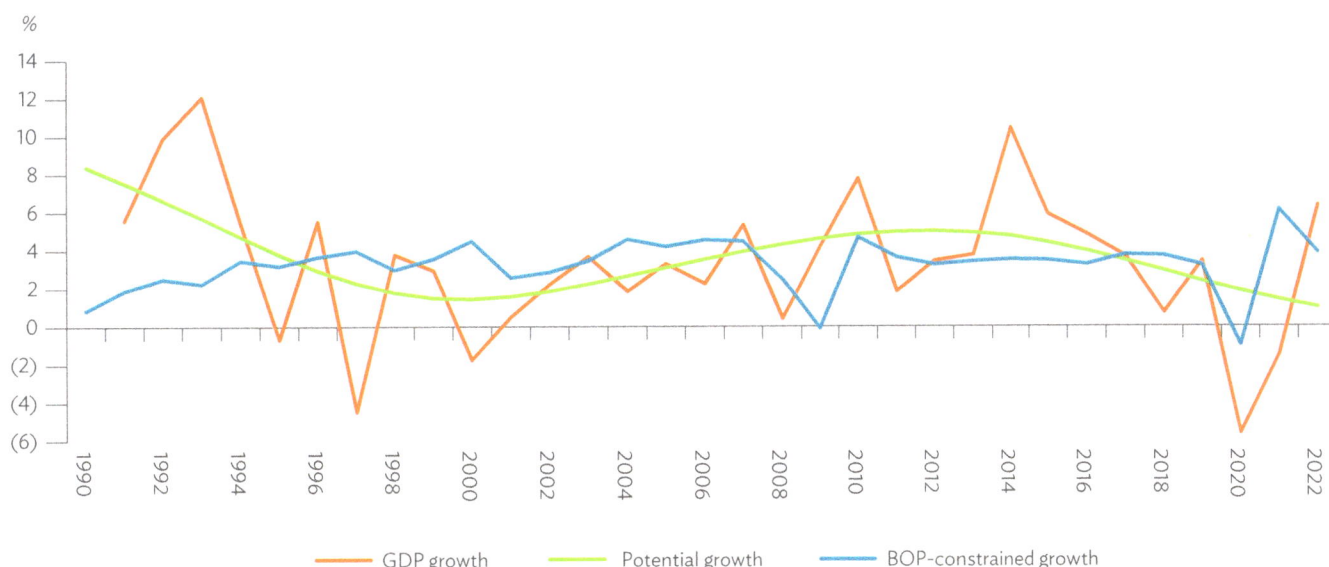

( ) = negative, BOP= balance-of-payments, GDP = gross domestic product.
Note: Potential growth is defined as the maximum GDP growth rate that is sustainable without creating inflationary pressures.
Source: Estimates derived from the State-Space model and based on the database of the United Nations Statistics Division (accessed June 2024).

Raising growth potential becomes more important in the Pacific subregion, which faces economic challenges due to supply chain disruptions caused by the COVID-19 pandemic and climate shocks. Even as Pacific DMCs recover from the impact of COVID-19, policymakers and governments recognize the need to strengthen fiscal fundamentals and maintain sufficient buffers to mitigate the adverse impacts of external demand shocks. Due to its small and undiversified economic base, limited infrastructure, and vulnerability to disasters and external shocks, the Pacific subregion has increased its import dependence. Unique challenges such as geographical remoteness from global markets and high transportation costs have impeded the subregion's ability to diversify its economic base. The Pacific subregion's vulnerability to disasters, external shocks, poor human capital stocks, and low productivity have led to a decline in the potential growth rate. These challenges constrain the ability of Pacific countries to achieve sustained and resilient growth.

With public resources stretched and fiscal space limited, the prospects of supporting inclusive and sustainable growth are further constrained. Economies must focus on improving public sector management, enhancing the quality of public service delivery, and creating room for private sector development. Boosting expenditure efficiency through improved project selection and enhancing development impact is crucial. These efforts necessitate the establishment of a solid human capital base to underpin productivity-led growth.

The pandemic highlighted the importance of strengthening institutions and making economies more resilient to future shocks. This involves improving banking and financial systems and implementing micro- and macro-prudential reforms. While research on the factors that determine economic resilience—defined as the speed at which countries recover from negative shocks—is inconclusive, one study (Abiad et al., 2009) suggests that countries with weak banking and financial systems due to inadequate supervision and ineffective macroprudential policies experienced larger output losses, mainly due to disruptions to credit supply that depressed investment rates. Lower investment rates, in turn, limit the productive capacity of the economy.

Considering the specific development challenges in the Pacific subregion, PFM reforms must consider the unique circumstances of Pacific economies. Given the limited capacity within these economies, the focus should be on identifying the most crucial reforms. For instance, improving budget planning can guide the prioritization of reforms, allowing for enhanced development impact under realistic resource constraints. Moreover, aligning budget allocations with development objectives is crucial for effective resource allocation.

Substantial disparities between budgeted allocations and actual spending at the input and functional levels can disrupt government priorities and compromise the budget's efficacy as a planning tool. In Pacific DMCs, optimizing the effectiveness of public expenditures necessitates minimizing deviations between planned and actual resource utilization to mitigate disruptions in public service delivery. Reforms should strive to align expenditure with the budget without imposing unmanageable burdens on available capacity or limiting flexibility when necessary and appropriate.

It is crucial to understand that PFM reforms present significant challenges and require substantial resources. Therefore, the accompanying road maps must carefully outline strategies for addressing capacity gaps. To effectively tackle Pacific DMCs' development obstacles, PFM reforms should explicitly include considerations and plans for evolving capacity requirements. Tailored approaches to bridging capacity gaps may be necessary, especially in nations grappling with pronounced capacity constraints. In addition to conventional capacity-building methodologies, Pacific DMCs should explore avenues for accessing capacity from non-traditional sources—including subregional institutions—and establish enduring collaborations with development partners, private enterprises, and individuals possessing the requisite proficiencies.

The unique development challenges facing the Pacific region require improvements in PFM, expenditure, and revenue systems. Reducing distortions in these areas can help create conditions that support long-term growth and economic resilience. Maintaining macroeconomic stability and strengthening PFM promote resilience and drive economic recovery. In the post-COVID-19 environment, Pacific DMCs must prioritize PFM reforms to improve the efficiency of their public sectors.

Examining the long-term growth trends in the Pacific region reveals a diminishing potential growth rate, predating the impact of COVID-19. The region's constrained growth is predominantly attributed to its lack of economic diversification and poor public sector management. This enduring constraint may be ascribed to the Pacific region's reliance on concessionary aid inflows and its imperative to uphold a manageable current account balance. To bolster economic resilience and cultivate more comprehensive and sustainable growth, the Pacific region must focus on introducing reforms to improve the quality of national institutions and the efficiency of economic structure. This underscores the critical role an effective public sector can assume in nurturing resilient growth through enhanced public financial management and high-quality public services.

Lead author: Kaukab Naqvi

Note

[1] The Pacific subregion in this policy note comprises the Cook Islands, Fiji, Kiribati, the Marshall Islands, the Federated States of Micronesia, Nauru, Niue, Palau, Papua New Guinea, Samoa, Solomon Islands, Tonga, Tuvalu, and Vanuatu. The subregional, balance-of-payments constrained, and potential GDP growth rates represent the weighted average growth of these economies.

References

A. Abiad et al. 2009. What's the Damage? Medium Term Output Dynamics after Banking Crises. IMF Working Paper. WP 09/245.

C. S. Adam and L. David. 2005. Fiscal deficits and growth in developing countries. *Journal of Public Economics*. 89. pp. 571–597.

A. Afonso et al. 2022. Twin deficit revisited: A role for fiscal institutions? *Journal of International Money and Finance*. 121.

B. Daniel and C. Si Gao. 2015. Implications of productive government spending for fiscal policy. *Journal of Economic Dynamics and Control*. 55. pp. 148–175.

B. Eichengreen, D. Park, and K. Shin. 2024. Economic resilience: Why some countries recover more robustly than others from shocks. *Economic Modelling*. 136.

X. Fengju and A. Wubishet. 2024. Analysis of the impacts of financial development on economic growth in East Africa: How do the institutional qualities matter? *Economic Analysis and Policy*. 82. pp. 1177–1189.

International Monetary Fund (IMF). 2015. Making Public Investment More Efficient. Policy Paper.

P. Jeasakul, C. Lim, and E. Lundback. 2014. Why Was Asia Resilient? Lessons from the Past and for the Future. IMF Working Paper. WP/14/38.

N. Jiang et al. 2024. Impact of financial reform on urban resilience: Evidence from the financial reform pilot zones in China. *Socio-Economic Planning Sciences*. 94.

P. Kannan, A. Scott, and M. Terrones. 2009. From Recession to Recovery: How Soon and How Strong? Unpublished manuscript. International Monetary Fund.

C. Reinhart and K. Rogoff. 2009. This Time Is Different: Six Centuries of Financial Folly. Princeton University Press.

A. P. Thirlwall. 1979. The Balance of Payments Constraint as an Explanation of International Growth Rate Differences. *Banca Nazionale del Lavoro Quarterly Review*. 128. pp. 45–53.

Understanding Vulnerability, Fragility, and Resilience in Pacific Small Island Developing States

SUMMARY

A sound understanding of a country's vulnerability and fragility helps us better support and build resilience. Vulnerability and fragility have structural, environmental, political-societal, economic, and institutional dimensions. The Asian Development Bank (ADB) is responding to growing vulnerability in the Pacific subregion by improving the diagnostic tools that provide context-specific analyses that contribute to country strategies and project approaches. Recognizing that some small island developing states (SIDS) also refer to themselves as "large ocean states"—emphasizing the vast exclusive economic zones and the central role oceans play in their economies, cultures, and environments—ADB aims to understand the unique opportunities and perspectives to strengthen resilience and improve the way it works toward sustainable development.

BACKGROUND

ADB adopted the *Fragile and Conflict-Affected Situations and Small Island Developing States Approach 2021–2025* (FSA) in June 2021.[1] The FSA outlines an operational approach and action plan for achieving the Strategy 2030 objectives to improve the effectiveness of its assistance toward development outcomes in (i) developing member countries (DMCs) that it classifies as experiencing fragility and/or conflict in various forms; (ii) self-identifying SIDS;[2] and (iii) subnational pockets of poverty and fragility.[3] The FSA complements the ADB *Pacific Approach 2021–2025*[4] and the country partnership strategies for Fiji and Papua New Guinea, which likewise focus on addressing prevailing fragilities and strengthening resilience.[5]

Based on its biennial country performance assessment (CPA) exercise, ADB uses an aggregate country classification system to identify the presence of fragility in its DMCs.[6] The CPA evaluates a country's policy and institutional framework to deliver intended development outcomes. However, this binary classification of whether a DMC is experiencing fragility provides insufficient insight into the context specificity; it also falls short in identifying the policy and investment support needed to help address the root causes and consequences of fragility. The FSA introduces a more nuanced conceptual understanding to guide and refine ADB support in fragile contexts (Figure 5).

ADB differentiates the fragility experienced by SIDS from that of larger DMCs where violence, conflict, and other fragilities may be the primary challenge; developing a specific approach to support its engagement, operations, and analytical understanding of vulnerability, fragility, and resilience (VFR) in these small and complex environments. Given the heightened risks that SIDS face primarily due to their unique challenges—and opportunities—the

approach to analyzing and understanding fragility in SIDS highlights vulnerability rather than fragility. Whereas fragility is defined as a combination of (i) exposure to risk and (ii) insufficient coping capacity of the state, system, or community to manage, absorb, or mitigate those risks, vulnerability refers more directly to the exposure or the condition(s) of being more susceptible to risk. Improving ADB's understanding of these conditions helps recognize existing resilience and understand the nuanced perspectives of SIDS on structural vulnerabilities that may lead to fragility. This leads to better-designed, context-specific interventions and aims to increase resilience in DMCs.

UNDERSTANDING VULNERABILITY AND FRAGILITY IN THE CONTEXT OF SIDS

There is a distinction between vulnerability and fragility based partially on the roots of these terms: the fragility concept stems from political science and international relations concerning the state's ability to act in society, whereas the vulnerability comes from economics, focused on the private sector and its ability to drive growth, and the exposure of an economy to withstand external shock such as a sudden currency or trade crisis. Nowadays, for SIDS, the term is also increasingly associated with environmental and political factors.

There are several forms of VFR encountered in SIDS:

(i)   The term fragility relates primarily to endogenous—internally derived—sources of weakness, while vulnerability relates to exogenous—external—shocks.

(ii) Sources of fragility differ in larger countries and small islands: in small islands, fragility tends not to be conflict-based and is not so much about state fragility per se. However, the language around fragility is often used interchangeably to describe failed states, which does not apply to most SIDS.

(iii) The relatively recent histories and legacies of colonialism and natural resource extraction in most Pacific SIDS help explain many factors leading to elevated vulnerability, including economic systems and forms of governance that disregard customary tradition and create challenges of dual governance systems and institutional structures.

(iv) Fixed geographical factors are critical determinants of vulnerability in SIDS, although how states and societies respond to these conditions is not fixed.

(v)   Small populations and geography limit the degree to which SIDS can diversify their economies and are key drivers of economic vulnerability.

(vi) International policies, institutions, and geopolitics can majorly impact SIDS' prosperity, with minimal scope for small islands to influence decisions that affect them.

Figure 5: ADB's Vulnerable Country Groups

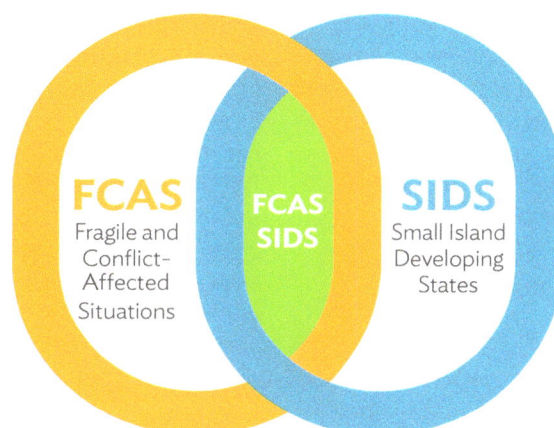

FCAS
Fragile and Conflict-Affected Situations

FCAS SIDS

SIDS
Small Island Developing States

Afghanistan	Federated States of Micronesia	Cook Islands
Lao People's Democratic Republic	Kiribati	Fiji
Myanmar	Marshall Islands	Maldives
	Nauru	Niue
	Palau	Samoa
	Papua New Guinea	Tonga
	Solomon Islands	Vanuatu
	Timor-Leste	
	Tuvalu	

Note: Effective 1 February 2021, ADB placed a temporary hold on sovereign project disbursement and new contracts in Myanmar. ADB placed its regular assistance to Afghanistan on hold effective 15 August 2021.
Source: ADB. 2021. *Fragile and Conflict-Affected Situations and Small Island Developing States Approach*.

(vii) Pacific countries are largely more remote and insular than other SIDS; as mostly low-lying islands, they are more exposed to sea-level rise; and have more multi-island territories, making the widespread provision of public goods complex and expensive.

(viii) Across SIDS, including the Pacific, there is huge diversity: many countries experience similar challenges linked to smallness, but they all have their own, usually complex patterns of VFR in both extent and nature.

In light of these key insights, ADB's fragility and resilience assessments (FRAs) approach to working in SIDS includes a deeper analytical dive into VFR's causes and consequences and recognizing the contextual specificity of each SIDS. Using FRAs as a diagnostic tool in the analytical process helps identify both the existing dimensions of VFR and externally driven processes that could exacerbate vulnerability and generate greater fragility in the future.

PACIFIC SIDS FRAS AND DIMENSIONS OF VULNERABILITY, FRAGILITY, AND RESILIENCE

The Pacific SIDS FRA approach assesses VFR capacity across six key dimensions: structural, environmental, economic, political,

societal, and institutional. This provides a structure to group similar aspects of vulnerability, yet also the flexibility to reflect the close interlinkages and connections between the dimensions. The section below outlines examples of VFR in each dimension, highlighting the points of intersection with economic vulnerability.

Structural vulnerability

In Pacific SIDS, structural vulnerabilities are pronounced. Immovable constraints include small size and population, remote location, and geographic dispersion, and narrow asset bases. While these structural dimensions of vulnerability cannot be overcome, they can be mitigated through targeted and context-specific interventions.

Structural vulnerability contributes to and is exacerbated by narrow-based economies—which results in low domestic resource mobilization from a limited domestic tax base in a small state environment—and very high costs in transport connectivity across the vast distances within some SIDS, which separate SIDS from international markets. Volatility in fossil fuel commodities negatively impacts Pacific SIDS to a disproportionate extent because of high dependence and cost.

Structural resilience

Paradoxically, while COVID-19 exposed Pacific SIDS' economic vulnerability, their remoteness became a source of resilience. Border closures effectively provided isolation against exposure and allowed time for vaccination before re-opening. Relatively small populations with high urban densities were possible to reach with vaccinations and public health messaging, and most Pacific SIDS were able to contain deadly outbreaks if not avoid them altogether.

Environmental vulnerability

Environmental vulnerability includes SIDS' high exposure to the negative effects of climate change (such as sea-level rise, ocean acidification, sea warming, and coastal erosion and inundation), disasters arising from natural hazards (including earthquakes, tsunamis, intense seismic activity), and the rising frequency and intensity of extreme weather events such as cyclones and king tides.

The impact of climate and natural hazard-driven events and the considerable costs involved in recovery contribute to governments' inability to effectively respond promptly, dragging on the economy and leading to unpredictable debt sustainability and constrained fiscal space. A lack of access to affordable market-based financing often compounds these challenges. A lack of creditworthiness hampers SIDS' access to finance, and for investors, the scale is often too small and risks too high to make SIDS attractive markets. SIDS governments must increasingly develop costly population displacement and relocation strategies as slower onset climate- and hazard-related impacts become a reality. Rapid urbanization stresses infrastructure, service provision, employment opportunities, and the environment.

Further, climate change impacts the critical income-generating sectors of tourism, fisheries, agriculture, and many secondary economic activities, including aquaculture, forestry, and ocean health, with further negative consequences for food security, nutrition, and livelihoods. SIDS are vulnerable to biodiversity loss and climate change because they lack economic alternatives. Despite the growing number of initiatives for global climate financing, access to securing this money has been prolonged, mainly due to complex application processes and eligibility requirements.

Environmental resilience

Strong biodiversity, natural resources, and innovation—including the potential for renewable energy—support economic growth and are thus important sources of resilience. A resurgence in traditional conservation methods and the use of local materials and practices to withstand natural hazards is increasingly being leveraged. However, most materials are still imported from abroad. SIDS lead on climate change action and play a strong advocacy role on the international stage to encourage partnerships and attract attention to the implications of climate change.

Economic vulnerability

The economic dimensions of VFR refer to the state's capacity to deliver sustainable economic growth with a shared distribution of benefits across the population. The susceptibility of SIDS to exogenous shock (global and/or regional economic downturn, health security, global commodity price fluctuation, and geopolitical factors) causes considerable uncertainty and adversely affects economic growth. Tourism-dependent economies are highly vulnerable to these shocks and climate- and natural hazard-driven crisis events for which recovery insurance options are scarce and costly. Recovery from shocks remains slow for some SIDS as the economic resources available are not commensurate with the scale of the task.

The high cost of import commodities, including fuel, drives an equally high cost of living in SIDS DMCs. Effective, affordable trade supported by open trade policies and enabling environments, trade agreements, and facilitation among the SIDS face the complexities and costs of vast ocean-exclusive economic zones compared with land-based border crossings that are more easily built into flourishing economic corridors and networks.

The private sector is still largely unable to support SIDS during an economic crisis and exogenous shock. Growth is constrained due to a weak enabling environment, where the government can crowd out private entrepreneurship as the largest employer and choose to hold key sectors under state-owned enterprises. There is a lack of access to finance for private firms, making it difficult for new players to enter and existing private enterprises to expand.

Economic resilience

Pacific SIDS have significant exclusive economic zones. If well managed, natural resources have important economic potential for existing sectors like fisheries and tourism and hold immense potential for many Pacific SIDS as the extractive capacity for critical minerals and seabed mining moves toward the implementation phase. Reducing fuel imports and building resilience through a just and inclusive transition to renewable energy is another way to build environmental and economic resilience. Economic diversification is a key strategy to build resilience, and some SIDS have established digital residency programs, digital currencies, and other innovations to capitalize on improved digital connectivity.

Political and societal vulnerability

These dimensions are mainly about access to and distribution of power, politics, people, and assets. While SIDS policy and institutional performance are drivers of vulnerability and thus fragility, several SIDS DMCs are also affected by a recent history of political and/or ethnic instability and, in some cases, intergroup conflict associated mainly with land, ocean, and natural resource ownership, access, and management.

While many SIDS have governance mechanisms that uphold traditional structures to an extent, these can sit uncomfortably with modern political systems that tend to reflect the legacies of colonialism rather than effectively build on and incorporate traditional endogenous forms of governance. As a result, customary practices of decision-making and consensus-building can be sidelined or diminished. They function in parallel to modern systems—especially related to land use and ownership—and contribute to frequent changes in government that negatively impact stability and growth. Small population sizes, a lack of inclusive representation in political roles, and dynastic or familial political succession building exacerbate these challenges. Weak judiciary systems and the rule of law are affected, as is corruption, which is a widespread challenge.

Geopolitical factors are outsized in Pacific SIDS, and there is growing competition and interest in the region. Pacific SIDS with free association agreements with other countries benefit from strengthened political, societal, and economic ties, but even these can be shaky; the level of commitment can be questioned when compact renewals are delayed. National dialogue on decolonization also seeks to reset colonial narratives by reclaiming traditional identity and considering name change.

Cultural traditions are strong and can provide robust societal resilience. However, the social fabric of Pacific SIDS is changing: domestic migration from rural to urban centers and international outmigration are shifting the balance in communities and diminishing the ability to depend on customary support networks. Traditional skills that ensured food security are being eroded by imported foodstuffs, leading to a severe increase in non-communicable diseases.

There is a high prevalence of sexual exploitation and gender-based violence against women in the Pacific, with often weak justice systems to enforce laws against perpetrators. Men dominate formal economic opportunities, and women remain a minority in leadership roles in both public and private sectors. This is despite many societies holding strong matrilineal traditions in their communities where women may have been responsible for family resources.

Political and societal resilience

Well-established regional mechanisms such as the Pacific Islands Forum and the Pacific Community strengthen SIDS' collective response to vulnerability and fragility. Some Pacific SIDS are strengthening political processes (Vanuatu) and stamping out corruption (Fiji). Traditional governance structures and social cohesion are important for societies, and some SIDS have adopted alternative measures for well-being as a counter to economic indicators alone. Families have a strong attachment to their land, an important source of resilience; those whose lands are threatened due to climate change are strong advocates for preservation and adaptation.

Institutional dimensions

Institutional dimensions refer to the effectiveness and integrity of governance. SIDS' relatively small population size can lead to weak governance, low institutional capacity, and the inability to deliver adequate public services across all sectors. This makes it challenging to build sufficient resilience to manage and mitigate risks.

The capacity gap in knowledge and skills continues to be challenging as financing requirements and administrative arrangements become more complex. The influx of resources for climate change will test the absorptive capacity of SIDS. Delivering public services across large swathes of the ocean in the case of archipelagic countries significantly increases costs and practical challenges. Political will and governance capacity to distribute financing equitably can be a risk whereby members of parliament cater to their constituencies where familial roots lie.

Labor migration is also eroding already low levels of institutional capacity. The loss of skilled labor in the domestic markets fuels uncertainty for the public and private sectors. Remittance flows to many SIDS present a more complex picture than in other DMCs, given permanent migration rights under various compacts of free association agreements (including labor mobility, residential rights, and/or citizenship) with countries such as Australia, New Zealand, and the United States. For some SIDS residents, outmigration instead creates an outflow of funds as children and older people need financial support for education or medical care abroad.

Institutional resilience

A significant opportunity exists for better coordination and stronger partnerships with development partners, SIDS governments, and regional institutions. Civil society, including the church, is an important part of society that provides essential services and disaster response, acting as de facto government in some areas, particularly in non-urban areas; chiefly, community systems and communities use traditional problem-solving methods and provide social safety nets.

INTERCONNECTED NATURE OF VULNERABILITY AND RESILIENCE

Using this multidimensional approach to understanding vulnerability and fragility disaggregates risk factors and facilitates a deeper analysis of their root causes. It is common for aspects to cross over between multiple dimensions as they intersect and interact. For example, while weak institutions may be a primary fragility, this may result from poor budget provisioning and/or vested interests preventing institutional reform, among other things. At a country-specific level, this understanding is important to developing strategies to address vulnerability and grow resilience.

Resilience-building must respond to both long- and short-term risks, which are both exogenous and endogenous and may also be latent or sudden. To address economic vulnerability, emphasis should be placed on both the way general SIDS vulnerabilities are heightened by the geography of Pacific SIDS and, in turn, induce and intensify patterns of fragility and how SIDS can and have leveraged their distinctive historical and sociocultural circumstances to develop and adapt unique resilience strategies to manage this predicament.

RESOURCES FOR ADB

Understanding the root causes and consequences of vulnerability and fragility is the first step to strengthening resilience in Pacific DMCs.

ADB has prepared practical resources to support country and project teams in diagnosing dimensions of vulnerability and fragility and applying them to program operations and interventions. These include the publication *A conceptual understanding of fragility and resilience in Asia and the Pacific*. At the same time, staff have further internal resources such as a *Handbook on preparing fragility and resilience assessments*, including an FRA template, and a *Guidance note on applying Differentiated Approaches in Country Partnership Strategies*. The FRA is a confidential document that the ADB resident mission country director holds. However, a Country Vulnerability, Fragility, and Resilience Profile is available for information and use by country and project teams.

Lead author: Erin Felton, senior operations coordination specialist (fragile and conflict-affected situations), Climate Change and Sustainable Development Department (CCSD), Asian Development Bank (ADB); and Rosalind McKenzie, principal operations coordination specialist (fragile and conflict-affected situations), CCSD, ADB.

Notes

[1]   ADB. 2021. *Fragile and Conflict-Affected Situations and Small Island Developing States Approach.*

[2]   SIDS are a group of 39 United Nations Members States and 18 Associate Members with similar development challenges. ADB acknowledges the preference of many SIDS for the term "big or large ocean state."

[3]   ADB. 2018. *Strategy 2030: Achieving a Prosperous, Inclusive, Resilient, and Sustainable Asia and the Pacific.* Paras. 26, 27, and 30.

[4]   The Pacific Approach covers 12 Pacific SIDS. ADB. 2021. *Pacific Approach 2021–2025.*

[5]   ADB. 2019. *Fiji: Country Partnership Strategy (2019–2023).* ADB. 2020. *Papua New Guinea: Country Partnership Strategy (2021–2025).*

[6]   A DMC is classified as FCAS if it has an average rating of 3.2 or less on ADB's country performance assessment (CPA) and the World Bank country policy and institutional assessment (CPIA). The classification also applies if a United Nations and/or regional peacekeeping or peace-building mission has been present in the country during the past 3 years.

References

ADB. 2023. *A Conceptual Understanding of Fragility in Asia and the Pacific.*

ADB. 2024. Guidance note on applying Differentiated Approaches in Country Partnership Strategies (internal).

ADB. Forthcoming. *FCAS and SIDS Annual Report 2023.*

ADB. 2023. Literature Review: Conceptualizing Fragility in Pacific Small Island Developing States: Unpublished.

Nonfuel Merchandise Exports from Australia
(A$; y-o-y % change, 3-month m.a.)

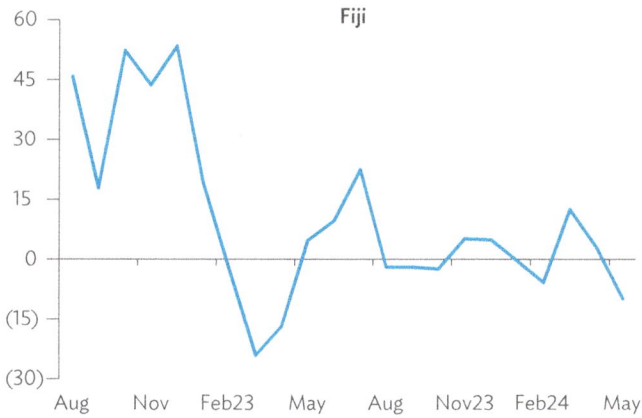

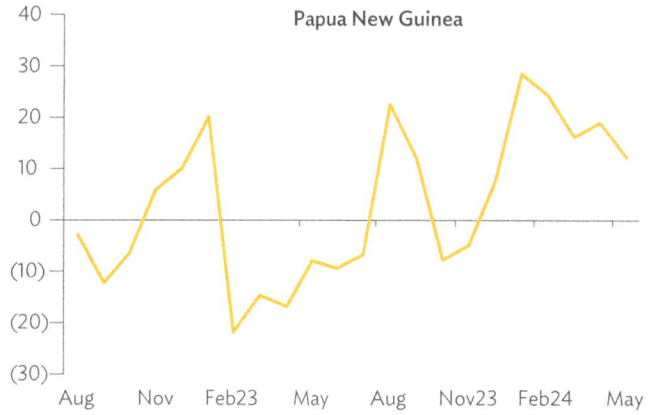

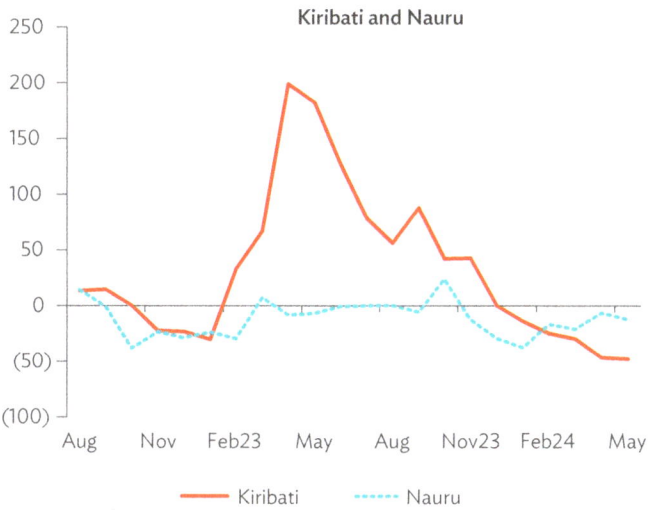

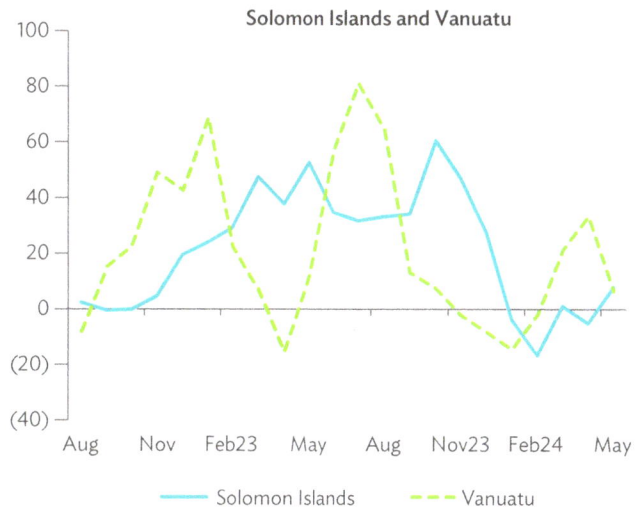

Fiji

Papua New Guinea

Kiribati and Nauru

—— Kiribati ---- Nauru

Solomon Islands and Vanuatu

—— Solomon Islands ---- Vanuatu

( ) = negative, A$ = Australian dollar, m.a. = moving average, y-o-y = year-on-year.

Source: Australian Bureau of Statistics.

Nonfuel Merchandise Exports from New Zealand and the United States
(y-o-y % change, 3-month m.a.)

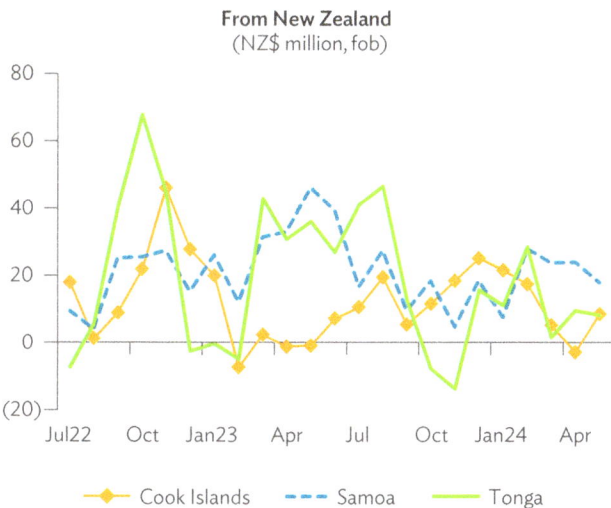

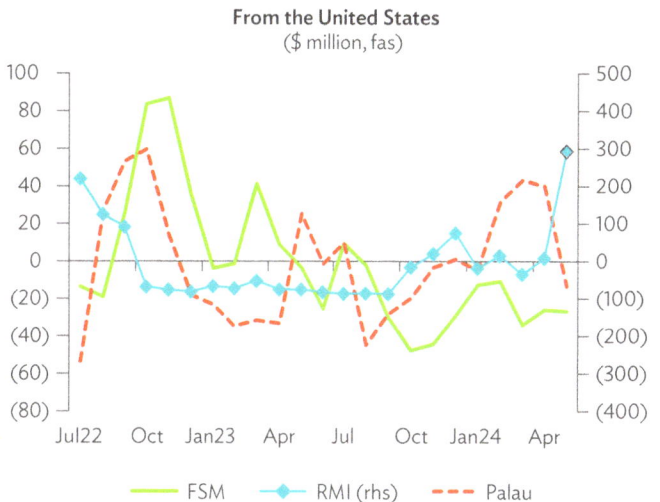

From New Zealand
(NZ$ million, fob)

From the United States
($ million, fas)

—◆— Cook Islands ---- Samoa —— Tonga

—— FSM —◆— RMI (rhs) ---- Palau

( ) = negative, fas = free alongside, fob = free on board, FSM = Federated States of Micronesia, m.a. = moving average, NZ$ = New Zealand dollar, rhs = right-hand scale, RMI = Republic of the Marshall Islands, y-o-y = year on year.

Sources: Statistics New Zealand and United States Census Bureau.

Diesel Exports from Singapore
(y-o-y % change, 3-month m.a.)

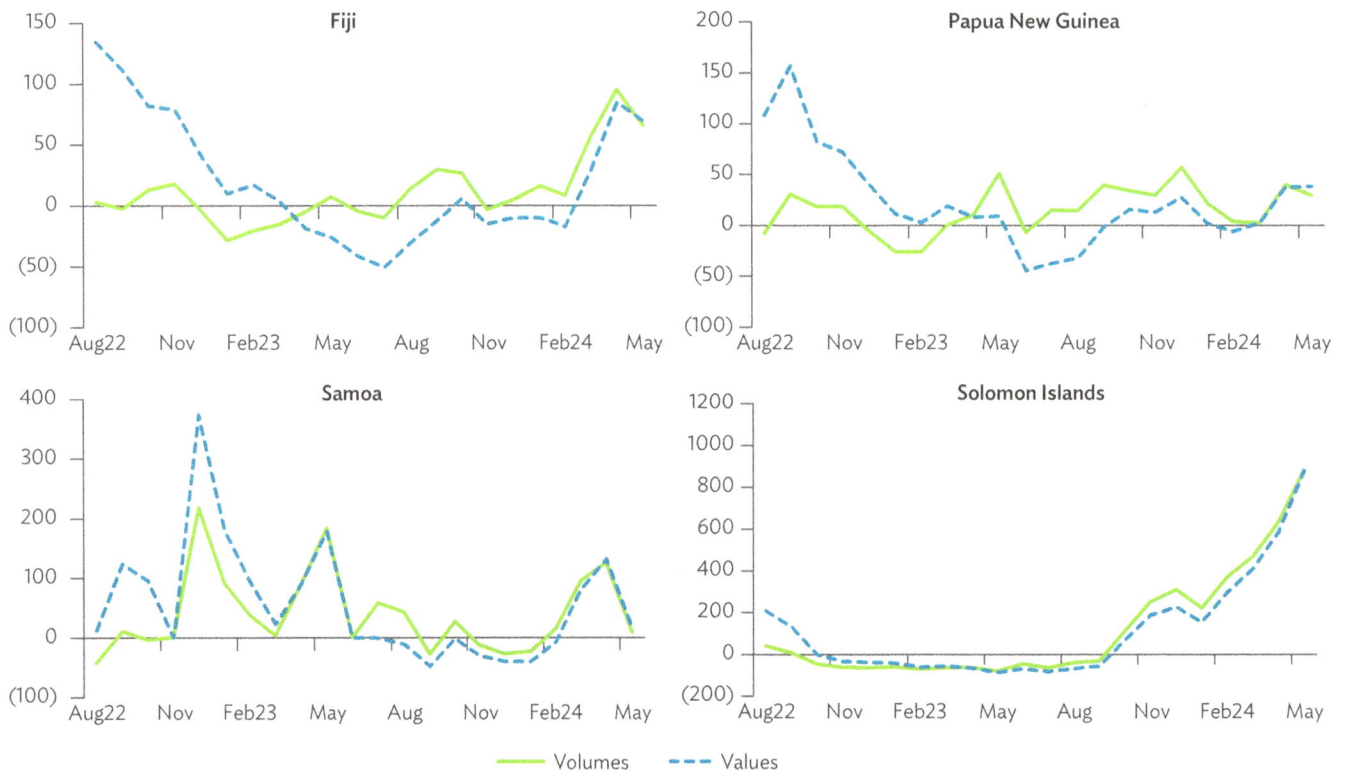

Fiji

Papua New Guinea

Samoa

Solomon Islands

—— Volumes - - - Values

( ) = negative, m.a. = moving average, y-o-y = year on year.
Source: International Enterprise Singapore.

Gasoline Exports from Singapore
(y-o-y % change, 3-month m.a.)

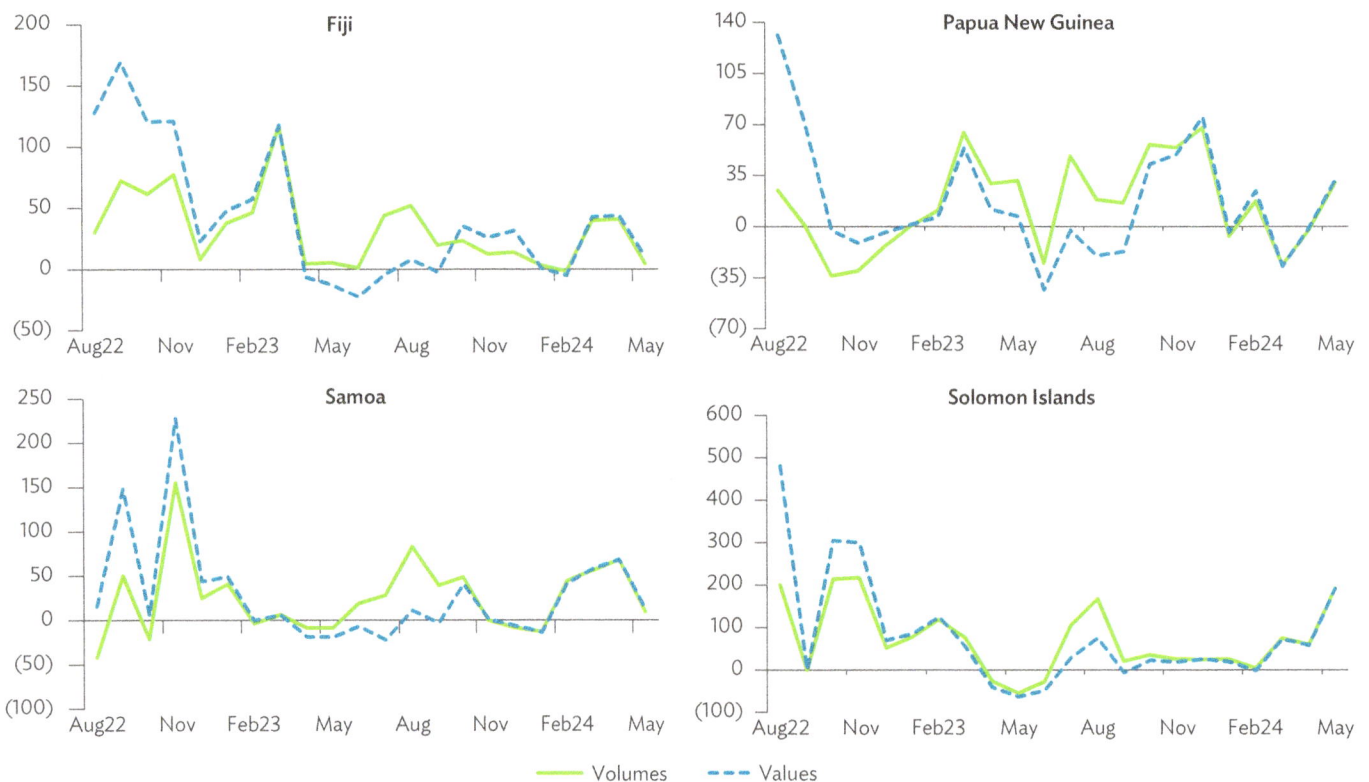

Fiji

Papua New Guinea

Samoa

Solomon Islands

—— Volumes - - - Values

( ) = negative, m.a. = moving average, y-o-y = year on year.
Source: International Enterprise Singapore.

Departures from Australia to the Pacific
(monthly)

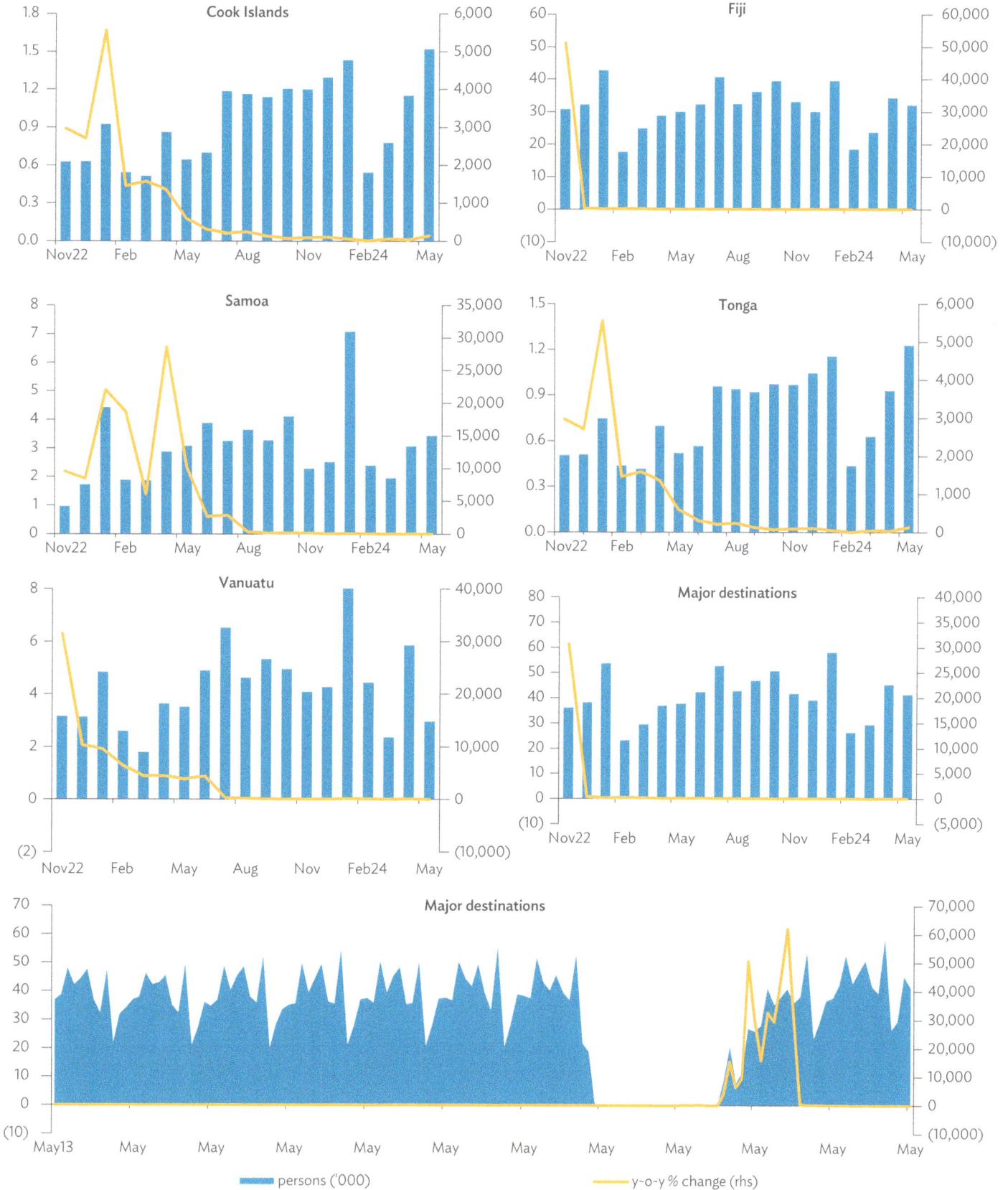

( ) = negative, rhs = right-hand scale, y-o-y = year on year.
Source: Australian Bureau of Statistics.

Departures from New Zealand to the Pacific
(monthly)

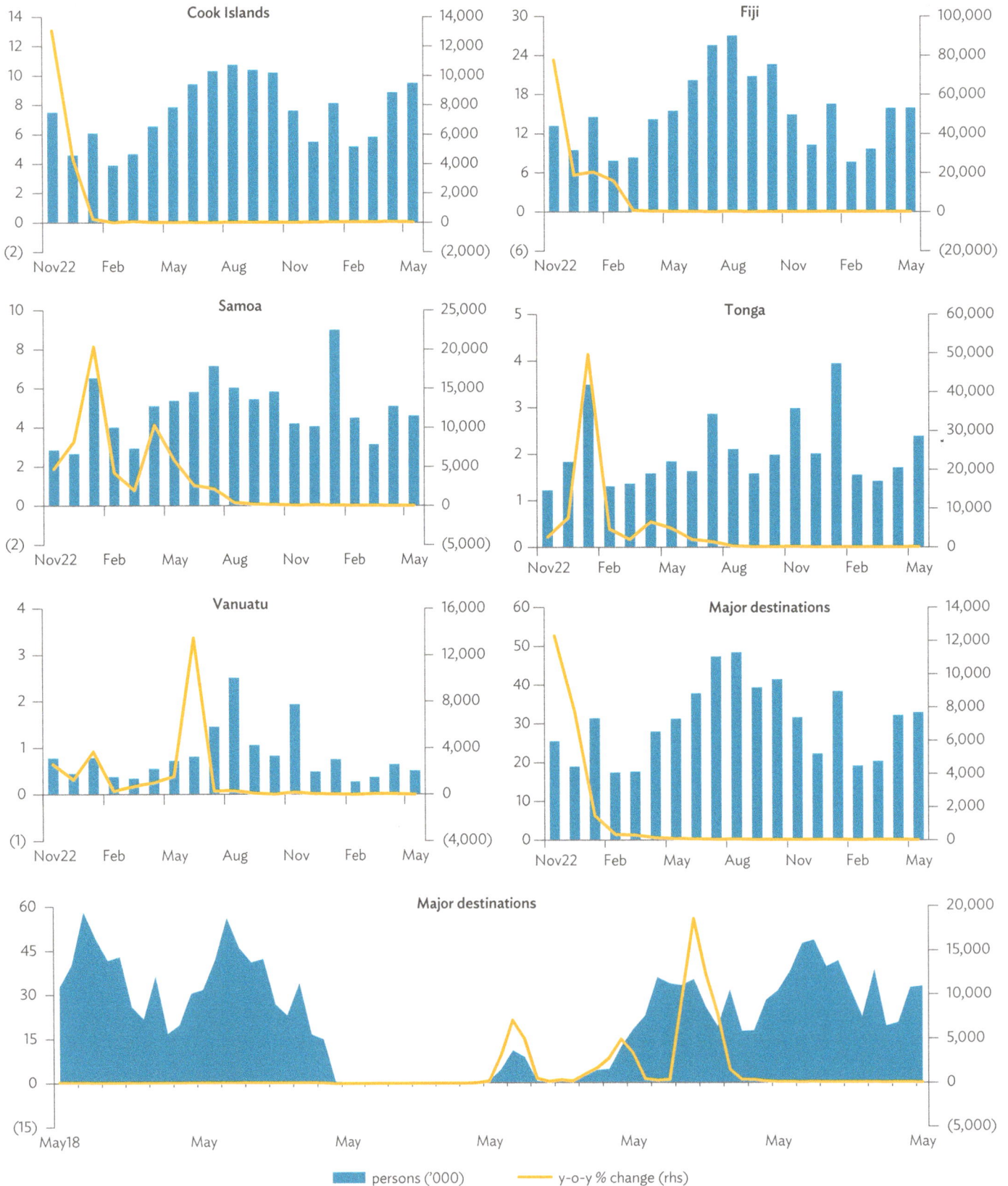

Cook Islands

Fiji

Samoa

Tonga

Vanuatu

Major destinations

Major destinations

persons ('000)　　　y-o-y % change (rhs)

( ) = negative, rhs = right-hand scale, y-o-y = year-on-year.
Source: Statistics New Zealand.